Penguin Books
Portuguese Phrase Book
Antonio de Figueiredo and Jillian Norman

Portuguese
Phrase Book

Antonio de Figueiredo and Jillian Norman

Penguin Books Ltd, Harmondsworth,
Middlesex, England
Penguin Books Inc., 7110 Ambassador Road,
Baltimore, Maryland 21207, U.S.A.
Penguin Books Australia Ltd, Ringwood,
Victoria, Australia
Penguin Books (N.Z.) Ltd,
182–190 Wairau Road,
Auckland 10, New Zealand

First published 1971
Reprinted 1973, 1976
Copyright © Jillian Norman and Antonio de Figueiredo, 1971

Made and printed in Great Britain by
Hazell Watson & Viney Ltd, Aylesbury, Bucks
Set in Monotype Plantin

CONTENTS

Introduction 7

Portuguese pronunciation 9

Essential grammar 15

First things 23
Essentials 23
Questions and requests 23
Useful statements 24
Language problems 25
Polite phrases 26
Greetings and hospitality 26

Signs and public notices 29

Money 31
Currency table 31

Travel 33
On arrival 33
Buying a ticket 34
Signs to look for at stations 35
By train and underground 36
By air 38
By ship 39
By bus or coach 40
By taxi 42

Directions 43

Motoring 45
At the garage 45
Road signs 46
Repairs 47
Parts of a car – vocabulary 49
Tyre pressure 53

Accommodation 54
Booking a room 54
In your room 56
At the porter's desk 58
Departure 59

Restaurant 61
Going to a restaurant 61
Ordering 62
Drinks 63
Paying 64
Breakfast 65
Restaurant vocabulary 65

The menu 69

Shopping 80
Where to go 80
In the shop 80
Choosing 81
Complaints 82
Paying 83
Clothes and shoes 84
Clothing sizes 85
Chemist 86
Toilet requisites 87
Photography 88
Food 89
Tobacconist 90
Newspapers, books, writing materials 91
Laundry and cleaning 92
Repairs 93

Barber and hairdresser 94

Post office 96

Letters and telegrams 96

Telephoning 97

Sightseeing 99

Entertainment 101

Sports and games 102

On the beach 104

Camping and walking 106

At the doctor's 108

At the dentist's 111

Problems and accidents 112

Time and dates 114

Public holidays 117

Numbers 118

Weights and measures 120

Vocabulary 125

INTRODUCTION

In this series of phrase books only those words and phrases that are essential to the traveller have been included. For easy reference the phrases are divided into several sections, each one dealing with a different situation. Some of the Portuguese phrases are marked with an asterisk – these attempt to give an indication of the kind of reply you may get to your questions, of questions you may be asked, or to indicate street signs and other notices that you should be aware of.

At the end of the book there is an extensive practical vocabulary list and here a pronunciation guide is given for each word. In addition there is an explanation of Portuguese pronunciation at the beginning of the book and a brief survey of the essential points of grammar. It would be advisable to read these sections before starting to use the book.

PORTUGUESE PRONUNCIATION

The pronunciation guide is intended for people with no knowledge of Portuguese. As far as possible the system is based on English pronunciation, but as Portuguese has an infinitely more complex sound structure, complete accuracy will sometimes be lost for the sake of simplicity. However, the reader should be able to understand Portuguese pronunciation and to make himself understood if he reads this section carefully. Each word in the vocabulary at the end of the book has a transcription into English symbols, according to the rules set out below.

Vowels

Pronounce			
a as **a** in father	symbol **ah**	fábrica – factory (fah-bree-ka)
as **a** in about or as **u** in put	symbol **a**	amigo – friend (a-mee-goo)
e, é as **e** in bet	symbol **e**	serra – mountain (ser-ra)
e, ê as **ay** in stay or as **ey** in they	symbol **ay, ai**	fazer – to do (fa-zair)
e, i as **e** in open or as **i** in bit	symbol **e**	antes – before (an-tesh)
(occurs only in an unstressed syllable, and as a final letter it is almost silent)			

i as **i** in machine	symbol **ee**	mil – thousand (meel)
Before a, e, o or u in unstressed syllables **i** resembles y in yes	symbol **y, ee**	férias – holiday (fer-ya)
o as **o** in olive	symbol **o**	bola – ball (bo-la)
o, ou, ô, final **oa** as **o** in so, most	symbol **oh**	ôvo – egg (oh-voo)
o as **oo** in boot (used in most unstressed syllables)	symbol **oo**	dormir – to sleep (door-meer)
Before stressed a, e, i, **o** resembles **w** in wet	symbol **w**	Coimbra (kwee^n-bra)
u as **u** in rule or **oo** in boot	symbol **oo**	usar – to use (oo-sar)
Before a, e, i and after o the **u** sound resembles **w** in wet	symbol **w**	água – water (a-gwa)

Diphthongs

Pronounce **ai** as **ie** in tie	symbol **i, y**	pai – father (py)
au as **ow** in how	symbol **ow**	causa – cause (kow-za)

oi, ói, as **oi** in oil or **oy** in boy (when o is stressed)	symbol **oy**	lençois – sheets (lay^n-soysh)

The other double vowels – **ei, éi, éu** – do not really have special sounds. They are very close to the sounds of the separate parts as listed above, and the same symbols are used.

e.g. comeis – you eat (koo-may-eesh); céu – sky (see-oo).

Nasals

These sounds should be made through the nose, but without pronouncing the 'n'. Nasalization is shown in spelling by a tilde over the vowel, or by an **m** at the end of a word, or by **m** or **n** before a consonant.

ã, am, an	symbol a^u	maçã – apple (ma-sa^n)
ẽ, em, en	symbol ay^n	cento – hundred (say^n-too)
im, in	symbol ee^n	cinco – five (see^n-koo)
õ, om, on	symbol o^n	bom – good (bo^n)
um, un	symbol oo^n	um – one (oo^n)
ão	symbol ow^n	pão – bread (pow^n)

| **ãe, ãi** | symbol y^n | mãe – mother (my^n) |
| **õe** | symbol oy^n | limões – lemons (lee-moy^{n}sh) |

Consonants

b, f, k, l, m, p, q, t, v are pronounced as in English, but note the following:

c before a, o, u or a consonant is pronounced **k**	symbol **k**	casa – house (kah-za)
c before e, i and ç are pronounced **s**	symbol **s**	certo – certain (serr-too)
ch is pronounced **sh** as in ship	symbol **sh**	chave – key (shahv)

d is softer than in English

| **g** before a, o, u is pronounced **g** as in got | symbol **g** | garfo – fork (gahr-foo) |

gu in combination gue, gui the u is not pronounced; its purpose is to keep the **g** hard, as above

| **g** before e, i is pronounced as **s** in pleasure | symbol **zh** | gente – people (zhay^n-tay) |

h is always silent

j is pronounced as **s** in pleasure	symbol **zh**	laranja – orange (lar-a^{n}zha)
lh is like **lli** in million	symbol **lly**	toalha – towel (too-a-llya)
nh is like **ni** in onion	symbol **ny**	vinho – wine (vee-nyoo)

r, rr is strongly trilled

s, ss at the beginning of a word or after a consonant is pronounced **s**	symbol **s**	saber – to know (sa-bair)
s between two vowels is pronounced **z**	symbol **z**	mesa – table (may-za)
s is pronounced as **sh** at the end of a word, and in certain other places or as	symbol **sh**	luvas – gloves (loo-vash)
s in pleasure	symbol **zh**	

w is like a stressed **v**

x is pronounced **sh** at the beginning or end of a word, and in certain other places	symbol **sh**	excelente – excellent (esh-say-lay^n-te)
as **z** in prefix **ex** before a vowel	symbol **z**	exacto – exact (ez-a-too)
as **s** between two vowels	symbol **s**	auxilio – help (ow-see-lyoo)
and occasionally as **ks**	symbol **ks**	táxi – taxi (tak-see)

y is pronounced as **i** in machine

z is pronounced as **z**	symbol **z**	azul – blue (az-ool)
as **sh** at the end of a word	symbol **sh**	faz favor – please (fash fa-vohr)

and sometimes as **s** in   symbol **zh**
pleasure

Stress

Words ending in the single vowels **a, e, o** or in **m** or **s** are stressed on
the last syllable but one: **fa**lo – I speak; **ca**sas – houses, ves**ti**do – dress.
In other words the stress usually falls on the last syllable: fa**lar** – to
speak; ma**çã** – apple; na**ção** – nation; ani**mal** – animal. Note that
nasal vowels and double vowels at the end of words do carry stress.
Exceptions to these rules are indicated by a written accent: café,
América. In the pronunciation guide used in the vocabulary words
with irregular stress have the stressed syllable printed in bold.

ESSENTIAL GRAMMAR

NOUNS

Nouns in Portuguese are either masculine or feminine.

Nouns denoting males, and most nouns ending in **-o** (except **-ção -são**) are masculine.

> e.g. tio – uncle; castelo – castle

Nouns denoting females, and those ending in **-a, ção, -são, -dade** are feminine.

> e.g. tia – aunt; cidade – city

There are exceptions to these rules.

> e.g. o coraçdo – heart

Plural

The plural is formed by adding **-s** if the word ends in a vowel.

Most words ending in a consonant add **-es** to form the plural.
> e.g. mulher (woman) – mulheres; luz (light) – luzes.

As a general rule nouns ending in **-al** become **-ais** in the plural.
> e.g. metal (metal) – metais; material (material) – materiais.

Nouns ending in **-ão** have varied forms in the plural.
> e.g. limão (lemon) – limões; instrucção (instruction) – instrucções; but pão (bread) – pães; cão (dog) – cães.

DEFINITE ARTICLE

o before a masculine singular noun	o banco (the bank)
os before a masculine plural noun	os bancos
a before a feminine singular noun	a mulher (the woman)
as before a feminine plural noun	as mulheres

INDEFINITE ARTICLE

um before a masculine singular noun   um barco (a ship)

uns before a masculine plural noun   uns barcos (some ships)

uma before a feminine singular noun   uma cadeira (a chair)

umas before a feminine plural noun   umas cadeiras (some chairs)

ADJECTIVES

Adjectives agree in gender and number with the noun.

Those ending in **-o** change to **-a** in the feminine.

> e.g. fresco – fresca (fresh, cool); cansado *of a man* – cansada *of a woman* (tired).

Those ending in **-e** and most of those ending in a consonant are the same in the masculine and the feminine.

> e.g. o castelo grande; a cadeira grande.

The plural is formed by adding **-s** if the word ends in a vowel, and **-es** in most cases when it ends in a consonant.

> e.g. fresco – frescos; grande – grandes; inglês – ingleses.

Adjectives ending in **-l** change the **-l** to **-is** or **-eis**.
> e.g. subtil – subtis (subtle).

The comparative and superlative are formed by putting **mais** before the adjective.

> e.g. um hotel barato   a cheap hotel
>
> um hotel mais barato   a cheaper hotel
>
> o hotel mais barato   the cheapest hotel

There are, however, exceptions to this rule: e.g. grande (big, great) becomes maior (bigger, greater).

POSSESSIVE ADJECTIVES

	m s	*m pl*	*f s*	*f pl*
my	meu	meus	minha	minhas
your *fam.*	teu	teus	tua	tuas
his, hers	seu/dele	sua/dela	seus/deles	suas/delas
our	nosso	nossa	nossos	nossas
your *fam.*	vosso	vossa	vossos	vossas
their, your *polite*	seu	sua	seus	suas

These adjectives agree with the thing possessed, e.g. meu pai (my father); meus pais (my parents); minha casa (my house), minhas casas (my houses); vosso livro (your book); vossas cartas (your letters).

PERSONAL PRONOUNS

	subject	*object*
I	eu	me
you *fam.*	tu	te
you *polite*	o senhor *m*	o
	a senhora *f*	a
he	ele	ele
she	ela	ela
we	nós	nos
you *fam.*	vós	vos
you *polite*	os senhores *m*	os
	as senhoras *f*	as
they *m*	eles	os
they *f*	elas	as

Personal pronouns are usually omitted before the verb.

e.g. vou – I go; vem – he (or she) comes.

Direct object pronouns are usually placed after the verb.

e.g. tenho-o – I have it.

Indirect object pronouns are the same as direct object pronouns except that **lhe, lha** are used to mean to it, to him, to her, to you (*polite*), and **lhes, lhas** mean to them, to you (*polite*).

e.g. dar-lhe – to give to him etc.; dar-lhes – to give to them.

If a direct and an indirect object pronoun are used together, the indirect one is placed first.

e.g. damo-vo-lo – we give it to you (vos + o becomes vo-lo).

If both pronouns are in the third person, **se** is used as indirect object.

e.g. se lho dâ – he gives it to him (her).

When speaking to strangers always use the form **o senhor, a senhora** and **os senhores, as senhoras**, with the verb in the third person. **Tu** and **você** are used to close friends and to children.

DEMONSTRATIVE PRONOUNS

this one, that one

	m	*f*
this (one)	êste	esta
these	êstes	estas
that (one)	êsse	essa
those	êsses	essas
that (one) over there	aquele	aquela
those over there	aqueles	aquelas

They agree in gender and number with the nouns they represent.

> e.g. êste é o meu bilhete – this is my ticket.
>   quero este livro, êsse, e aquele – I want this book,
>   that one and that one over there.

The demonstrative adjectives have the same form as the pronouns.

VERBS

'To be' is translated by **ser** and **estar**.
When it is followed by a noun, or when it indicates an origin, or a permanent or inherent quality, **ser** is used.

> e.g. a neve é fria e branca   snow is cold and white
>   sou Britanico   I am British
>   a Inglaterra é parte duma ilha England is part of an island

When it indicates position or a temporary state, **estar** is used.

> e.g. o carro está na rua principal the car is in the main street
>   estamos em Portugal   we are in Portugal

Present tense of **ser** and **estar**

	ser	*estar*
I am	sou	estou
you are *fam.*	és	estás
you are *polite*	é	está
he, she is	é	está
we are	somos	estamos
you are	sois	estais
they, you are	são	estão

In Portuguese there are three types of regular verbs, distinguished by the endings of the infinitives.

e.g. **-ar** falar – to speak
     -er vender – to sell
     -ir partir – to leave, go away

The *present tense* is formed as follows:

falar	vender	partir
falo	vendo	parto
falas	vendes	partes
fala	vende	parte
falamos	vendemos	partimos
falais	vendeis	partis
falam	vendem	partem

The imperfect tense

falar	vender
falava – *I spoke, have spoken, was speaking, etc.*	vendia – *I sold, have sold, was selling, etc.*
falavas	vendias
falava	vendia
falávamos	vendíamos
faláveis	vendíeis
falavam	vendiam

Verbs ending in **-ir** (partir) have the same endings in the imperfect as those in **-er** (vender).

The irregular imperfect tense of **ser** – to be

era
eras
era
éramos
éreis
eram

The present and imperfect tenses of some common irregular verbs:

dar – *to give*		dizer – *to say*		fazer – *to do, make*	
dou	dava	digo	dizia	faço	fazia
dás	davas	dizes	dizias	fazes	fazias
dá	dava	diz	dizia	faz	fazia
damos	dávamos	dizemos	dizíamos	fazemos	fazíamos
dais	dáveis	dizeis	dizíeis	fazeis	fazíeis
dão	davam	dizem	diziam	fazem	faziam

ir – *to go*		poder – *can, to be able*		saber – *to know*	
vou	ia	posso	podia	sei	sabia
vais	ias	podes	podias	sabes	sabias
vai	ia	pode	podia	sabe	sabia
vamos	íamos	podemos	podíamos	sabemos	sabíamos
ides	íeis	podeis	podíeis	sabeis	sabíeis
vão	iam	podem	podiam	sabem	sabiam

ter – *to have*		ver – *to see*		vir – *to come*	
tenho	tinha	vejo	via	venho	vinha
tens	tinhas	vês	vias	vens	vinhas
tem	tinha	vê	via	vem	vinha
temos	tínhamos	vemos	víamos	vimos	vínhamos
tendes	tínheis	vêdes	víeis	vindes	vínheis
têm	tinham	vêem	viam	vêm	vinham

The future is formed by adding the following endings to the infinitives of all regular verbs:

falar	vender	partir
falar**ei**	vender**ei**	partir**ei**
falar**ás**	vender**ás**	partir**ás**
falar**á**	vender**á**	partir**á**
falar**emos**	vender**emos**	partir**emos**
falar**eis**	vender**eis**	partir**eis**
falar**ão**	vender**ão**	partir**ão**

The present tense of **ir** – to go, can also be used to form the future, as in English.

> e.g. vou comprar um guia – I'm going to buy a guide book, I shall buy a guide book.

The negative is formed by putting **não** before the verb.

> e.g. não falo português – I don't speak Portuguese.

FIRST THINGS

Essentials

Yes	Sim
No	Não
Please	Por favor/faz favor
Thank you	Obrigado
No thank you	Não, obrigado

Questions and requests

Where is/are . . .?	Onde está/estão . . .?
When?	Quando?
How much is/are . . .?	Quanto é/são . . .
How far?	Qual é a distância?
What's that?	O que é aquilo?
What do you want?	O que deseja?
What must I do?	O que devo fazer?
Have you . . .?	Têm . . .?
Is/are there . . .?	Há . . .?

Have you seen . . .?	Viu . . .?
Please give me . . .	Faça o favor de me dar . . .
I want/should like . . .	Quero . . .

Useful statements

I like it	Gosto
I don't like it	Não gosto
I'm not sure	Não tenho a certeza
I don't know	Não sei
I didn't know	Não sabia
I think so	Penso que sim
I'm hungry	Tenho fome
I'm thirsty	Tenho sede
I'm tired	Estou cansado/a
I'm in a hurry	Estou com pressa
I'm ready	Estou pronto/a
Leave me alone	Deixe-me por favor
Just a moment	* Um momento
This way, please	* Por aqui/siga-me

Take a seat	* Sente-se
Come in	* Entre
It's cheap/expensive	É barato/caro
It's too much	É demasiado
That's all	É tudo
You're right	Tem razão
You're wrong	Não tem razão

Language problems

I'm English/American/ South African	Sou inglês/americano/sul-africano (inglesa/americana/ sul-africana)
Do you speak English?	Fala inglês?
I don't speak Portuguese	Não falo português
I don't understand	Não entendo/compreendo
Would you say that again please?	Repita isso por favor
Please speak slowly	Fale lentamente por favor

Polite phrases

Sorry/excuse me	Desculpe
That's all right	Está bem
Not at all/don't mention it	De nada
Don't worry	Não se preocupe
It doesn't matter	Não importa
I beg your pardon?	O quê/Como disse?
Am I disturbing you?	Incomodo?
I'm sorry to have troubled you	Desculpe tê-lo incomodado
Good/that's fine	Bem/está bem

Greetings and hospitality

Good morning/good day	Bom dia
Good afternoon	Boa tarde
Good evening/good night	Boa noite
Hello	Olá
How are you?	Como está

Very well, thank you	Muito bem obrigado
Good bye	Adeus
See you soon	Até logo
May I introduce you to my wife/husband	Vou apresentá-lo(la) à minha/meu mulher/marido
Glad to know you	Encantado
What's your name?	Como se chama?
Where are you from?	Donde é você?
What's your address/telephone number?	Qual é a sua direção/o seu número de telefone?
Where are you staying?	* Onde está hospedado/a?
Are you doing anything this evening?	Está comprometido/a esta noite?
Could we have coffee/dinner together?	Poderíamos tomar café/jantar juntos?
Would you like to go to the museum/cinema/dancing with me?	Gostaria de ir a um museu/ao cinema/ou clube noturno comigo?
Would you like a drink/cigarette?	* Quere beber alguma coisa/quere um cigarro?
Help yourself	* Sirva-se
Can I offer you anything?	* Posso oferecer-lhe alguma coisa?
Thanks for a pleasant time	Muito obrigado pela sua hospitalidade

Thanks for the invitation	Muito obrigado pelo seu convite
Remember me to ...	Saudades a .../cumprimentos a ...
Bon voyage	Boa viagem
Good luck/all the best	Boa sorte

SIGNS AND PUBLIC NOTICES[1]

Aberto	Open
Agua potável	Drinking water
Alugam-se quartos	Rooms to let
Ascensor/elevador	Lift/elevator
Banco	Bank
Caixa	Cash desk/cashier
Cautela/precaução	Caution
Cavalheiros/senhores	Gentlemen
Chamar/chamada	Knock/ring
Circulem pela direita	Keep right
Correios	Post office
Direcção proibida	No entry
Entrada	Entrance
Entrada gratuita	Admission free
É proibido fumar	No smoking
É proibida a entrada	No admission
Fechado	Closed
Guia	Guide
Há quartos	Vacancies/rooms to let
(Hotel) completo	No vacancies
Informação	Information
Intérprete	Interpreter

1. See also Road Signs (p. 46), and Signs at Stations etc. (p. 35).

Lavabos	Lavatory
Livre	Vacant/free/unoccupied
Não há lugares	House full (cinema etc.)
Não pisar a relva	Keep off the grass
Não tocar	Do not touch
Ocupado	Engaged/occupied
Particular	Private
Pede-se para não ...	You are requested not to ...
Peões	Pedestrians
Perigo	Danger
Polícia	Police
Proibido ... sob multa de ...	Trespassers will be prosecuted
Reservado	Reserved
Retretes	Lavatory
Saída	Exit
Saída de emergência	Emergency exit
Senhoras	Ladies
Senhores	Gentlemen

MONEY

Is there an exchange bureau[1] near here?	Há alguma casa de câmbio perto de aqui?
Do you cash travellers' cheques?	Trocam cheques de viagem?
Where can I cash travellers' cheques?	Onde posso trocar cheques de viagem?
I want to change some English/South African/American money	Quero trocar dinheiro inglês/sul africano/americano
How much do I get for a pound/dollar?	A quanto está a libra/o dolar?
Can you give me some small change	Dê-me algum dinheiro trocado, por favor
Sign here please	*Assine aqui por favor
Go to the cashier	*Vá à caixa

Currency table

The currency is the escudo, and 100 centavos = 1 escudo. The escudo is represented by the symbol $ placed between the escudos and the centavos (e.g. 1$50 = one escudo, fifty centavos).

1. Portuguese banks are open from 09.30 to 12.00 and from 14.00 to 16.00 hrs, Monday to Friday. On Saturdays from 09.30 to 11.30 hrs. Exchange bureaux are open from 09.30 to 18.00 Monday to Friday and 09.30 to 13.00 on Saturdays.

1 escudo	= 2p	1 escudo	= 3 cents
5 escudos	= 9p	5 escudos	= 17 cents
10 escudos	= 18p	10 escudos	= 34 cents
50 escudos	= 91p	50 escudos	= $1.70
100 escudos	= £1.82	100 escudos	= $3.42
500 escudos	= £9.10	500 escudos	= $17.15
1,000 escudos or 1 conto	= £18.20	1,000 escudos	= $34.29
£1	= 55 escudos	$1	= 30 escudos

1 escudo	= 2 cents
5 escudos	= 12 cents
10 escudos	= 25 cents
50 escudos	= R1.25
100 escudos	= R2.50
500 escudos	= R12.50
1,000 escudos	= R25
R1	= 39$95

These rates of exchange are approximate only and subject to variation.

TRAVEL

On Arrival

Customs	* Alfândega
Passport control	* Contrôle de passaportes
Your passport, please	* O passaporte, por favor
May I see your green card card please?	* Pode mostrar-me o certificado de seguro?
Are you together?	* Viajam juntos?
I'm travelling alone	Viajo só
I'm travelling with my wife/a friend	Viajo com a minha esposa/um amigo
I'm here on business/on holiday	Venho em negócios/de férias
What is your address in Lisbon?	* Qual é a sua direcção em Lisboa?
How long are you staying here?	* Quanto tempo vai estar aqui?
How much money have you got?	* Quanto dinheiro traz?
I have . . . escudos/pounds/ dollars	Tenho . . . escudos/libras/ dolares
Which is your luggage?	* Qual é a sua bagagem?
Have you anything to declare?	* Tem algo a declarar?
This is my luggage	Esta é a minha bagagem
I have only my personal things in it	Tenho sómente as minhas coisas pessoais

Open your bag, please	* Abra a mala, por favor
Can I shut my case now?	Posso fechar já a mala?
May I go through?	Já posso passar/posso ir-me embora?
Where is the information bureau, please?	Onde está o bureau de informação, por favor?
Porter, here is my luggage	Bagageiro (moço) esta é a minha bagagem
What's the price for each piece of luggage?	Qual é o preço por cada mala?
I shall take this myself	Eu levo esta
That's not mine	Essa não é minha
Would you call a taxi?	Pode chamar-me um taxi?
How much do I owe you?	Quanto lhe devo?

Buying a ticket[1]

Have you a timetable, please?	Tem um horário, por favor?
How much is it first class to . . . .?	Quanto custa um bilhete de primeira para . . .?

1. You can buy a kilometric ticket for journeys of a minimum of 1,500 kilometers within Portugal. Application for such a ticket should be made to any principal Portuguese station at least a week before the journey commences.

First and second class travel are available on most trains, and on certain express trains a supplement is payable.

A second/third class to ...	Um bilhete de segunda/terceira para ...
A return to ...	Um bilhete de ida e volta a ...
A book of tickets, please[1]	Uma carteira de bilhetes
How long is this ticket valid?	Por quanto tempo é válido este bilhete?
Is there a supplementary charge?	Há que pagar algum suplemento?

Signs to look for at stations, termini, etc.

Arrivals	Chegadas
Booking office	Bilheteira
Buses	Autocarros
Connections	Correspondência
Departures	Partidas
Enquiries	Informações
Gentlemen	Cavalheiros/Senhores
Ladies	Senhoras
Left luggage	Depósito de bagagem (consigna)

1. This is only available for underground journeys.

Lost property	Secção de objectos perdidos
No smoking	É proibido fumar
Refreshments	Bar/snack-bar
Reservations	Reservas
Suburban lines	Carreiras suburbanas
Taxi rank	Paragem de taxis
Tickets	Bilhetes
Underground	Metro
Waiting room	Sala de espera

By train and underground [1]

RESERVATIONS AND ENQUIRIES

Where's the railway station?	Onde é a estação de caminho de ferro?
Two seats on the 11.15 tomorrow to . . .	Duas reservas para amanhã no comboio das onze e um quarto para . . .
I want to reserve a sleeper	Quero reservar uma cama

1. For help in understanding the answers to these and similar questions see TIMES (p. 114), NUMBERS (p. 118), DIRECTIONS (p. 43).

I want to register this luggage through to . . .	Quero despachar esta bagagem com destino a . . .
Is it an express?[2]	E rápido?
Is there an earlier/later train?	Há um comboio mais cedo/ mais tarde?
Is there a restaurant car on the train?	Há carruagem restaurante?

CHANGING

Is there a through train to . . .?	Há comboio directo a . . .?
Do I have to change?	Tenho que fazer mudança?
When is there a connexion to . . .?	Quando se muda para ir a . . .?

DEPARTURE

When does the train leave?	A que horas parte o comboio?
Which platform does the train to . . . leave from?	De que plataforma sai o comboio para . . .?
Is this the train for . . .?	É este o comboio para . . .?

ARRIVAL

When does it get to . . .?	A que horas chega a . . .?
Does the train stop at . . .?	O comboio pára em . . .?
How long do we stop here?	Quanto tempo paramos aqui?

2. Express trains are called *rápidos* and stopping trains *comboios-correios*.

Is the train late?	Está atrasado o comboio?
When does the train from ... get in?	A que horas chega o comboio que vem de ...?
At which platform?	Em que plataforma?

ON THE TRAIN

We have reserved seats	Temos lugares reservados
Is this seat free?	Está livre este lugar?
This seat is taken	Este lugar está ocupado

By air

Where's the airline office?	Aonde são os escritórios da companhia de aviação?
I'd like to book two seats on Monday's plane to ...	Quero marcar dois bilhetes para segunda-feira para o avião de ...
Is there a flight to Oporto on Thursday?	Há algum vôo na quinta-feira para o Porto?
Are there night flights to ...?	Há vôos nocturnos para ...?
When does it leave?	A que horas parte o avião?
When does it arrive?	A que horas chega o avião?

When's the next plane?	A que horas é o próximo avião?
Is there a coach to the airport?	Há autocarro para o aeroporto?
When must I check in?	A que horas me devo apresentar?
Please cancel my reservation to ...	Quero anular a minha reserva para ...
I'd like to change my reservation to ...	Quero mudar a minha reserva para ...

By ship

Is there a boat from here to ...?	Há barco de aqui para ...?
How long does the boat take?	Quanto tempo leva?
How often does the boat leave?	De quanto em quanto tempo sai o barco?
Where does the boat put in?	Em que portos toca?
Does the boat call at ...?	O barco toca em ...?
When does the next boat leave?	A que horas sai (parte) o próximo barco?
Can I book a single berth cabin? a first class/second-class/luxury class cabin?	Posso reservar um camarote individual?/um camarote de primeira/de segunda/de luxo?

How many berths are there in this cabin?	Quantas camas há nêste camarote?
When must we go on board?	A que horas há que estar a bordo?
When do we dock?	A que horas atracamos?
How long do we stay in port?	Quanto tempo ficamos no porto?

By bus or coach

Where's the bus station/coach station?	Aonde é a estação de autocarros/camionetas?
Bus stop	Paragem de autocarros
Request stop	Paragem facultativa
When does the coach leave?	A que horas parte a camioneta?
When does the coach get to...?	A que horas chega a camioneta a ...?
What stops does it make?	Em que sítios pára?
How long is the journey?	Quanto tempo é a viagem?
We want to take a coach tour round the sights	Queremos visitar os sítios de interesse em autocarro turístico

Is there an excursion to . . . tomorrow?	Há amanhã alguma excursão a . . .?
Does this bus go to the town centre/beach/station?	Vai êste autocarro para o centro da cidade/para a praia/para a estação?
When's the next bus?	A que horas é o próximo autocarro?
How often do the buses run?	De quanto em quanto tempo há autocarros?
Has the last bus gone?	Já partiu o último autocarro?
Do you go near . . .?	Este autocarro passa perto de . . .?
Where can I get a bus to . . .?	Onde posso tomar o autocarro para . . .?
Which bus goes to . . .?	Que autocarro vai a . . .?
I want to go to . . .	Quero ir a . . .
Where do I get off?	Onde tenho que apear-me/sair-me?
The bus to . . . stops over there	* O autocarro para . . . pára alí
A number 30 goes to . . .	* O número trinta vai para . . .
You must take a number 24	* Tem de tomar o número vinte e quatro
You get off at the next stop	* Sai na próxima paragem
The buses run every ten minutes/every hour	* Há autocarros de dez em dez minutos/de hora a hora

By taxi

Are you free?	Está livre?
Please take me to the Ritz hotel/the station/this address	Ao hotel Ritz /à estação /a esta direcção por favor
Can you hurry, I'm late?	Pode ir mais depressa por favor, estou atrasado
I want to see the sights/main streets	Quero ver os sítios de interesse/as ruas principais
Please wait for me here	Espere aqui por favor
Stop here	Pare aqui
Is it far?	É longe?
How much do you charge by the hour/for the day?	Quanto leva por hora/por dia?
How much will you charge to take me to . . .?	Quanto me levaria para ir a . . .?
How much is it?	Quanto é?
That's too much	É demasiado (é muito caro)

DIRECTIONS

Where is . . .?	Onde é . . .?
How do I get to . . .?	Como se vai para . . .?
How far is it to . . .?	A que distância fica . . .?
How many kilometres?	Quantos quilómetros?
How do we get on to the motorway to . . .?	Como se vai para a autoestrada de . . .?
Which is the best road to . . .?	Qual o melhor caminho para . . .?
Is it a good road?	É uma boa estrada?
Is there a motorway?	Há autoestrada?
Will we get to . . . by evening?	Chegaremos a . . . antes de anoitecer?
Where are we now?	Onde estamos agora?
Please show me on the map	Indique-me-o no mapa, por favor
It is that way	* É por ali
It isn't far	* Não é longe
Follow this road for 5 kilometres	* Siga uns cinco quilómetros nesta estrada
Keep straight on	* Siga em frente
Turn right at the crossroads	* Volte à direita no cruzamento
Take the second road on the left	* Tome a segunda estrada à esquerda
Turn right at the traffic-lights	* Volte à direita nos sinais luminosos

Turn left after the bridge

The best road is the ...

Take the ... and ask again

* Volte à esquerda depois da ponte

* A melhor estrada é a ...

* Tome a ... e pergunte novamente

MOTORING

Where can I hire a car?	Onde posso alugar um carro?
I want to hire a car and a driver/self-drive car	Quero alugar um carro com conductor/sem conductor
How much is it to hire it by the hour/day/week?	Quanto custa o aluguer à hora/dia/semana?
Have you a road map?	Tem um mapa de estradas?
Where is there a car park?	Onde há um parque de estacionamento?
Can I park here?	Posso estacionar aqui?
How long can I park here?	Por quanto tempo posso estacionar aqui?
May I see your licence, please?	* A sua carta de condução por favor?

At the garage

Where's the nearest petrol station?	Onde é a estação de gasolina mais próxima?
How far is the next service station?	A que distância é a próxima estação de serviço?
30 litres of petrol, and please check the oil and the water	Trinta litros de gasolina e reveja o óleo e a água, por favor
Fill her up please	Encha-o, por favor
How much is petrol a litre?	Quanto custa um litro de gasolina?

The oil needs changing	O óleo necessita ser mudado
Check the tyre pressure, please	Verifique o ar, por favor
Please change the wheel	Mude a roda, por favor
This tyre is flat/punctured	Esta câmara de ar está vazia/furada
The valve is leaking	A válvula perde ar
The radiator is leaking	O radiador perde água
Please wash the car	Lave o carro, por favor
Can I leave the car here?	Posso deixar o carro aqui?
What time does the garage close?	A que horas fecha a garagem?

Road signs

Circulação pela direita/esquerda	Keep right/left
Curvas	Winding road, bends
Descida acentuada (íngreme)	Steep hill
Desvio	Diversion
Direcção proibida	No entry
É proibido estacionar, estacionamento proibido	No parking
Estrada cortada	Road blocked

Estrada estreita	Narrow road
Guiar com cuidado	Drive with care
Parar	Stop
Passagem proibida	Overtaking prohibited
Perigo	Danger
Sentido proibido	No through road
Sentido único	One way street
Trabalhos de estrada	Road works
Trânsito vedado	Road closed
Velocidade limitada	Speed limit

Repairs

Is there an Austin agent here?	Há aqui uma agência Austin?
Have you a breakdown service?	Há serviço de reparações de emergência?
Is there a mechanic?	Há um mecânico?
My car's broken down, can you send someone to tow it?	O meu carro está avariado, pode mandar-me um reboque?
I want the car serviced	Quero uma revisão
The battery is flat, it needs charging	A bateria está em baixo, precisa de ser carregada

My car won't start	O meu carro não arranca
It's not running properly	Não anda bem
The engine is overheating	O motor está demasiado quente
The engine knocks/is firing badly	O motor está a bater/funciona mal
It's smoking	Está deitando fumo
Can you change this faulty plug?	Pode mudar-me esta vela defeituosa?
There's a petrol/oil leak	Perde gasolina/óleo
There's a smell of petrol/rubber	Cheira a gasolina/borracha
There's a rattle	Há um ruido
Something is wrong with my car/the engine/the lights/the clutch/the gearbox/the brakes/the steering	Há algo que não está bem no meu carro/o motor/as luzes/a embreagem/a caixa das velocidades/os travões/a direcção
This doesn't work	Isto não funciona
The oil warning light is on	Tem pouco óleo
The carburettor needs adjusting	O carburador precisa de um ajuste
Can you repair it?	Podem repará-lo?
How long will it take to repair?	Quanto tempo necessita para repará-lo?
What will it cost?	Quanto custará?
When will the car be ready?	Quando estará pronto o carro?

I need it as soon as possible/in three hours/in the morning	Preciso dêle o mais cedo possível/dentro de três horas/ pela manhã
It will take two days	* Demorará dois dias
We can repair it temporarily	* Pode-se reparar provisòriamente
We haven't the right spares	* Não temos as peças sobressalentes necessárias
We have to send for the spares	* Temos que pedir as peças sobressalentes
You will need a new . . .	* Vai precisar de um novo . . ./ uma nova . . .

Parts of car and other vocabulary useful in a garage

accelerate (to)	acelerar
accelerator	o acelerador
anti-freeze	o anti-congelante
axle	o eixo
battery	a bateria
bonnet	a capota
boot/trunk	a mala

brake	o travão
bumper	o pára-choques
carburettor	o carburador
choke	o estrangulador
clutch	a embreagem
crank-shaft	a manivela
cylinder	o cilindro
differential-gear	o diferencial
dip stick	o indicador de nível de óleo
distributor	o distribuidor
door	a porta
doorhandle	o manípulo da porta
drive (to)	conduzir
driver	o condutor
dynamo	o dínamo
engine	o motor
exhaust	o tubo de escape
fan	a ventoínha
fanbelt	a correia da ventoínha
flat tyre	a câmara de ar vazia/ o pneu vazio
foglamp	o farol de nevoeiro
fusebox	a caixa dos fusíveis
gasket	a junta de culatra

gears	as mudanças
gear-box	a caixa de velocidades
gear-lever	a alavanca de velocidades
grease (to)	lubrificar
handbrake	o travão de mão
horn	a buzina
ignition	a ignição
ignition key	a chave de ignição
indicator	o indicador
jack	o macaco
lights-head/side/rear	os faróis/o pisca-pisca/as luzes trazeiras
mirror	o espelho
numberplate	a chapa de matrícula
nut	a porca
oil	o óleo
petrol	a gasolina
petrol can	o depósito de gasolina
piston	o piston
plug	a vela
points	os pontos/pontas
propellor shaft	o veio de transmissão
puncture	o furo
radiator	o radiador

reverse	a marcha atrás
seat	o assento
shock absorber	o amortecedor
silencer	o silenciador
spares	os sobressalentes
spare wheel	a roda sobressalente
sparking plug	a vela de ignição
speedometer	o conta-quilómetros
spring	a mola
stall (to)	enguiçar
starter	o arranque
steering	a direcção
steering wheel	o volante
tank	o depósito
transmission	a transmissão
tyre	o pneu
valve	a válvula
wheel	a roda
window	a janela
windscreen	o pára-brisas
windscreen washers	os lava pára-brisas
windscreen wipers	os limpa pára-brisas

Tyre pressure

lb. per sq. in.	kg. per sq. cm.	lb. per sq. in.	kg. per sq. cm.
16	1·1	36	2·5
18	1·3	39	2·7
20	1·4	40	2·8
22	1·5	43	3·0
25	1·7	45	3·1
29	2·0	46	3·2
32	2·3	50	3·5
35	2·5	60	4·2

A rough way to convert lb. per sq. in. to kg. per sq. cm.: multiply by 7 and divide by 100.

ACCOMMODATION[1]

Booking a room

Rooms to let/vacancies	* Alugam-se quartos/há quartos vagos
No vacancies	* (Hotel) completo
Have you a room for the night?	Tem um quarto para esta noite?
Do you know another good hotel?	Pode recommendar-me um outro bom hotel?
I've reserved a room; my name is ...	Tenho um quarto reservado; o meu nome é ...
I want a single room with a shower	Quero um quarto individual com duche
We want a room with a double bed and a bathroom	Queremos um quarto de casal e casa de banho
Have you a room with twin beds?	Tem um quarto com duas camas?
I want a room with a washbasin	Quero um quarto com lavabo
Is there hot and cold water?	Há água quente e fria?
I want a room for two or three days/a week/until Friday	Quero um quarto para dois ou três dias/uma semana/até sexta-feira

1. See also LAUNDRY (p. 92) and RESTAURANT (p. 61).
In addition to privately owned hotels and pensions Portugal also has state owned country inns called *pousadas*. The maximum stay in a *pousada* is limited to five days. *Estalagens* are small hotels.

What floor is the room on?	Em que andar é o quarto?
Is there a lift/elevator?	Há elevador?
Have you a room on the first floor?	Tem um quarto no primeiro andar?
May I see the room?	Posso ver o quarto?
I'll take this room	Fico com este quarto
I don't like this room	Não gosto deste quarto
Have you another one?	Tem outro?
I want a quiet room	Quero um quarto sossegado
There's too much noise	Há muito barulho
I'd like a room with balcony	Desejaria um quarto com terraço
Have you a room looking on to the street/the sea?	Tem um quarto que dê para a rua/o mar?
We've only a twin-bedded room	* Temos só quartos de duas camas
This is the only room vacant	* Este é o único quarto vago
We shall have another room tomorrow	* Teremos outro quarto amanhã
The room is only available tonight	* O quarto só está vago por esta noite
How much is the room per night?	* Quanto custa o quarto por noite?
Have you nothing cheaper?	Não tem nada mais barato?
Is the service included?	O serviço está incluído?

Are meals included?	As refeições estão incluídas?
How much is the room without meals?	Quanto é o quarto sem refeições?
How much is full board/half board?	Quanto é a pensão completa/ meia pensão?
Do you do bed and breakfast?	Tem quarto com pequeno almoço?

In your room

I'd like breakfast in my room, please	Quero o pequeno almoço no meu quarto, por favor
Please wake me at 8.30	Chame-me às oito e meia, por favor
There's no ashtray in my room	Não há cinzeiro no meu quarto
Can I have more hangers, please?	Podem dar-me mais cabides, por favor?
Is there a point for an electric razor?	Há tomada para máquina de barbear?
What's the voltage?[1]	Qual é a voltagem?

1. The most usual types of current in Portugal are 110 and 220 volts.

Where is the bathroom?	Onde é a casa de banho?
Where is the lavatory?	Onde é a retrete?
Is there a shower?	Há chuveiro?
There are no towels in my room	Não há toalhas no meu quarto
There's no soap	Não há sabão
There's no water	Não há àgua
There's no plug in my washbasin	Não há válvula no meu lavatório
There's no toilet paper in the lavatory	Não há papel higiénico na retrete
The washbasin is blocked	O lavabo está entupido
The lavatory won't flush	O autoclismo não funciona
May I have another blanket/ another pillow?	Pode me arranjar outra manta/ outra almofada?
The sheets on my bed haven't been changed	Não mudaram os lençois da minha cama
I can't open my window, please open it	Não consigo abrir a janela, pode abrí-la por favor
It's too hot/cold	Faz bastante calor/frio
Can the heating be turned up/ down?	Pode abrir/fechar o aquecimento um pouco mais?
Can the heating be turned on/ off?	Pode abrir/fechar o aquecimento?
Is the room air-conditioned?	O quarto tem ar condicionado?

The air conditioning doesn't work	O ar condicionado não funciona
Come in	Entre
Put it on the table, please	Ponha em cima da mesa, por favor
I'd like these shoes cleaned	Quero estes sapatos limpos
Could you get this dress/suit cleaned up a bit?	Podem-me limpar um pouco este vestido/fato?
I want this suit pressed	Quero este fato passado
When will it be ready?	Quando estará pronto?
It will be ready tomorrow	* Estará pronto amanhã

At the porter's desk

My key, please	A chave do meu quarto, por favor
Are there any letters for me?	Há alguma carta para mim?
Are there any messages for me?	Há alguma mensagem para mim?
If anyone phones, tell them I'll be back at 4.30	Se alguém me telefonar digam que eu volto às quatro e meia

No one telephoned	* Ninguém telefonou
There's a lady/gentleman to see you	* Há uma senhora/um senhor perguntando por si
Please ask her/him to come up	Por favor, diga-lhe para subir
I'm coming down at once	Desço imediatamente
Have you any writing paper/ envelopes/stamps?	Tem papel de carta/envelopes/ selos?
Please send the chambermaid	O empregado de quarto, por favor
I need a guide/interpreter	Necessito um guia/um intérprete
Where is the dining room?	Onde é a sala de jantar?
What time is breakfast/lunch/ dinner?	A que hora é o pequeno almoço/o almoço/o jantar?
Is there a garage?	Tem aqui garagem?
Is the hotel open all night?	O hotel está aberto toda a noite?
What time does it close?	A que horas fecha?

Departure

I am leaving tomorrow	Saio amanhã
Can you have my bill ready?	Pode tirar-me a conta?

I shall be coming back on . . ., can I book a room for that date?

Regressarei no dia . . ., posso reservar um quarto para essa data?

Could you have my luggage brought down?

Pode trazer a minha bagagem para baixo?

Please order a taxi for me at 11 o'clock

Chame-me um taxi para as onze horas, por favor

Thank you for a pleasant stay

Muito obrigado por tão agradável estadia

RESTAURANT

Going to a restaurant[1]

Can you suggest a good restaurant/a cheap restaurant/ a vegetarian restaurant?	Pode recomendar-nos um bom restaurante/um restaurante económico/um restaurante vegetariano?
I'd like to book a table for four at 1 o'clock	Queria reservar uma mesa para quatro, para a uma hora
I've reserved a table; my name is ...	Tenho uma mesa reservada; o meu nome é ...
Have you a table for three?	Há uma mesa para três?
Is there a table free on the terrace?	Há uma mesa livre no terraço?
This way, please	* Por aqui, se faz favor (por favor)
We shall have a table free in half an hour	* Haverá uma mesa livre dentro de meia hora
We don't serve lunch until 1	* Não se servem almoços até à uma hora
We don't serve dinner until 8 o'clock	* Não se servem jantares até as oito horas
We stop serving at 2 o'clock	* Acabamos de servir às duas horas

1. In Portugal lunch is usually served between 12.30 and 14.00 and dinner from 19.30 to 21.30.

Where is the lavatory?	Onde é a retrete? (o w.c.)
It is downstairs	* É em baixo/É ao fundo das escadas
We are in a (great) hurry	Temos (muita) pressa
Do you serve snacks?[2]	Servem pratos combinados?

Ordering

Waiter/waitress *to call*	Criado/criada
May I see the menu, please?	O menu/a ementa, por favor
May I see the wine list, please?	A lista dos vinhos, por favor
Is there a set menu?	Há menu do dia/menu turístico?
What do you recommend?	O que aconselha?
Can you tell me what this is?	Pode dizer-me o que é isto?
What is the speciality of the restaurant?	Qual é a especialidade da casa?
What is the speciality of the region?	Qual é o prato típico da região?
Would you like to try . . .?	* Quere provar . . .?

2. A *prato combinado* is a main dish served in bars and cafés. It consists of various types of meat, vegetables, fish, eggs, etc., in a number of different combinations.

There's no more ...	* Já não há ...
I'd like ...	Quero ...
May I have peas instead of beans?	Pode dar-me ervilhas em vez de feijão?
Is it hot or cold?	Este prato é quente ou frio?
This isn't what I ordered, I want ...	Isto não é o que pedi, eu quero ...
Without oil/sauce, please	Sem azeite/molho, por favor
Some more bread, please	Mais pão, por favor
A little more ...	Um pouco mais ...
This is bad	Está mau
This is undercooked	Está pouco cozido
This is stale	Está passado
This is tough	Está duro

Drinks

What will you have to drink?	* O que desejam beber?
A bottle of the house wine, please	Uma garrafa de vinho da casa
Do you serve the wine by the glass?	Servem vinho a copo?

Three glasses of beer, please	Três cervejas, por favor
Do you have draught beer?	Tem cerveja de barril?
Two more beers	Mais duas cervejas
I'd like another glass of water, please	Outro copo de água, por favor
The same again, please	O mesmo novamente, por favor
Three black coffees and one with milk	Três cafés e um café com leite
I want to see the head waiter/ manager	Quero ver o chefe dos criados/o encarregado
May we have an ashtray?	Pode dar-nos um cinzeiro, por favor?
Can I have a light, please?	Pode dar-me lume, por favor?

Paying

The bill, please	A conta, por favor
Please check the bill – I don't think it's correct	Reveja a conta, por favor, penso que não está certa
I didn't have soup	Não comi sopa
I had chicken, not lamb	Comi galinha, não carneiro
May we have separate bills	Pode dar-nos a conta em separado

Breakfast

A large white coffee/a black coffee, please	Um café com leite duplo/um café, por favor
I would like tea with milk/lemon	Quero chá com leite/limão
May we have some sugar, please?	Pode dar-nos açúcar?
A roll and butter	Pão com manteiga
Toast	Torradas
More butter, please	Mais manteiga, por favor
Have you some jam?	Tem alguma compota?
I'd like a soft-boiled/hard-boiled egg	Eu queria um ovo quente/cozido
What fruit juices have you?	Que sumos de fruta têm?

Restaurant vocabulary

ashtray	o cinzeiro
bar	o bar
beer	a cerveja

P.P.B. – 3

bill	a conta
bottle/half a bottle	a garrafa/meia garrafa
bread	o pão
butter	a manteiga
carafe	a jarra de vinho
cigarettes	os cigarros
cigar	o charuto
cloakroom	o vestiário
coffee	o café
course/dish	o prato
cup	a chávena
fork	o garfo
glass	o copo
hungry (to be)	ter fome
jug of water	a jarra de água
knife	a faca
lemon	o limão
matches	os fósforos
mayonnaise	a mayonnaise
menu	o menu/a lista/a ementa
milk	o leite
mustard	a mustarda
napkin	o guardanapo
oil	o azeite

pepper	a pimenta
plate	o prato
restaurant	o restaurante
salt	o sal
sandwich	a sande/sanduiche
toasted sandwich	a sande-torrada
sauce	o molho
saucer	o pires
service	o serviço
snacks	os pratos ligeiros
spoon	a colher
sugar	o açúcar
suggestion/recommendation	a sugestão/recomendação
table	a mesa
table cloth	a toalha de mesa
tea	o chá
terrace	o terraço
thirsty (to be)	ter sede
tip	a taxa de serviço/gorgeta
toothpick	o palito
vegetarian	o vegetariano
vinegar	o vinagre
waiter	o empregado de mesa

waiter *to call*	criado/criada
waitress	a empregada de mesa
water	a água
wine	o vinho
wine list	a lista de vinhos

THE MENU

SOPAS	SOUPS
Açorda	garlic and bread
Caldo	consommé
Caldo de galinha	chicken consommé
Caldo de rabo de boi	oxtail
Caldo verde	green cabbage (Portuguese variety)
Sopa de cebola	onion
Sopa de galinha	chicken
Sopa de mariscos	shellfish
Sopa de massa	noodle
Sopa de peixe	fish
Sopa de tomates	tomato
Sopa de verduras/legumes	vegetable

HORS D'OEUVRES	HORS D'OEUVRES
Alcachofras	artichokes
Anchovas	anchovies
Arenques	herring
Azeitonas	olives
Biqueirões	fresh anchovies
Caracois	snails
Espargos	asparagus
Fiambre	(smoked) ham

Gambas	prawns
Melão	melon
Ostras	oysters
Ovos	eggs
Perceves	goose barnacles
Salada	salad
Sardinhas	sardines

PEIXE	FISH
Ameijoas	clams
Atum	tunny
Bacalhau	dried salt cod
Bacalhau à Gomes de Sà	dried cod with potatoes, onions and garlic
Bacalhau cozido com batatas/grão	stewed cod (unspiced) with potatoes/chick peas
Besugo	sea bream
Bolinhos de bacalhau	cod fish cakes
Caldeirada de peixe *payshe*	fish stew
Caranguejo (de mar)	crab
Caranguejo (de rio)	crayfish
Chere, chernio	grouper
Choco, calamar	squid
Chocos com tinta	squid cooked in their own ink
Enguias	eels

Gambas	prawns
Goraz	bream
Lagosta	lobster
Lampreia	lamprey
Linguado	sole
Mexilhão	mussels
Peixe espada	swordfish
Peixe frito	mixed fried fish
Pescada	hake
Polvo	octopus
Raia	skate
Robalo	turbot
Salmão	salmon
Salmonete	red mullet
Sardinhas	sardines
Sardinhas assadas	grilled sardines
Sardinhas de escabeche	pickled sardines

CARNE	MEAT
Almôndegas	meatballs/rissoles in a spicy sauce
Borrego	mutton
Carneiro	lamb
Carneiro assado	roast lamb

Carne assada (de vaca)	roast beef
Chouriço	sausage made from spiced, cured pig meat
Costeleta	chop
Enchidos	sausages
Escalope	escalope
Feijoada	beans and meat
Fígado	liver
Filetes de carne	fillet of beef
Guisado de vitela	braised veal
Leitão	sucking pig
Linguiça	spiced sausage
Língua	tongue
Lombo	loin
Miolos	brains
Morcela	spiced blood sausage
Pé de porco	pig's trotters
Presunto	smoked ham
Rabo de vaca (boi)	oxtail
Rins	kidneys
Salpicão	smoked, spiced pork
Salsicha	sausage
Toucinho	bacon
Vaca	beef
Vitela	veal

Vitela assada	roast veal
Vitela estufada	veal stew

AVES E CAÇA	POULTRY AND GAME
Cabrito	kid
Coelho	rabbit
Faisão	pheasant
Galinha	chicken
Galinha piri-piri	chicken with a seasoning made from dried red chillies and olive oil
Galinhola	woodcock
Galo	cock
Ganso	goose
Javali	boar
Lebre	hare
Pato	duck
Pato bravo	wild duck
Perdiz	partridge
Peru	turkey
Pombo	pigeon

ARROZ	RICE
Arroz de bacalhau	rice with salt cod

Arroz de caril	curry and rice
Arroz de galinha	rice with chicken
Arroz de peixe	rice with fish
LEGUMES E VERDURAS	VEGETABLES
Aipo	celery
Alcachofra	artichoke
Alface	lettuce
Alho	garlic
Arroz	rice
Azeitonas	olives
Batatas	potatoes
Batatas assadas	roast potatoes
Batatas cozidas	boiled potatoes
Batatas fritas	fried potatoes
Beringela	aubergine, eggplant
Beterraba	beetroot
Cebola	onion
Cenoura	carrot
Cogumelos	mushrooms
Couve	cabbage
Couve de Bruxelas	Brussels sprouts
Couve-flor	cauliflower
Ervilhas	peas

Espargos	asparagus
Espinafres	spinach
Favas	broad beans
Feijão	beans
Nabo	turnip
Pepino	cucumber
Pimento	pepper
Rábanos	radishes
Salada	salad
Salsa	parsley
Tomate	tomato

OVOS	EGGS
Omeleta	omelette
Omeleta de batata	potato omelette
Omeleta de espargos	asparagus omelette
Ovos com presunto	ham and eggs
Ovos cozidos	boiled eggs
Ovos cozidos duros	hard-boiled eggs
Ovos escalfados com torradas	poached eggs on toast
Ovos fritos	fried eggs
Ovos mexidos	scrambled eggs
Ovos quentes cozidos moles	soft boiled eggs

SOBREMESA	DESSERT
Compota	preserved fruit
Filhós	fritters
Flan	crème caramel
Gelado	ice cream
Gemas de ovos	candied egg yolks
Merengue	meringue
Pastel/tarta	cake
Torrão	kind of nougat

FRUTAS FRESCAS E SECAS	FRUIT AND NUTS
Alperce	apricot
Amêndoa	almond
Amendoim	peanut
Ananás	pineapple
Avelã	hazel nut
Banana	banana
Cereja	cherry
Figo	fig
Laranja	orange
Limão	lemon
Maçã	apple
Melancia	water melon
Melão	melon

Morango	strawberry
Noz	walnut
Papaia	papaya
Passa	raisin
Pera	pear
Pêssego	peach
Tâmara	date
Toranja	grapefruit
Uva	grape
BEBIDAS	DRINKS
Água	water
Água gasosa de soda	soda water
Água mineral	mineral water
Água termal	thermal water
Bebidas alcoólicas	alcoholic drinks
Brande/aguardente	brandy
Cacau	cocoa
Café	coffee (black)
Café com leite	white coffee
Cerveja	beer
Chá	tea
Chá gelado com limão	iced tea with lemon
Champanhe	champagne

Chocolate quente	hot chocolate
Conhaque	cognac
Laranjada	orangeade
Leite (quente)	(hot) milk
Licor	liquor
Limonada	lemonade, lemon-squash
Sumos	juices
Sidra	cider
Vinho	wine
branco	white
da Madeira	Madeira
doce	sweet
do Porto	Port
espumante	sparkling
rosé	rosé
seco	dry
tinto	red
verde	light wine, made from not fully matured grapes

COOKING METHODS

assado	roast
bem passado	well done
cru	raw

frito	fried
guisado	braised
grelhado	grilled
mal passado	rare

SHOPPING

Where to go

Where are the best department stores?	Aonde são os melhores armazéns?
Which are the best shops?	Quais são as melhores lojas?
Where is the market/ supermarket?	Onde é o mercado/ super-mercado?
Is there a market every day?	Há mercado todos os dias?
Where's the nearest chemist?	Onde é a farmácia mais próxima?
Can you recommend a hairdresser?	Pode recomendar-me um cabeleireiro?
Where can I buy ...?	Onde posso comprar ...?
When are the shops open?[1]	Quando abrem as lojas?

In the shop

Self service	* Self service
Sale (clearance)	* Saldo
Cash desk	* Caixa

1. Shops are open from 09.00 or 09.30 to 13.00 and from 15.00 to 19.00 or 20.00 hrs.

Shop assistant	O empregado
Manager	O gerente/o responsável
Can I help you?	* Que deseja?
I want to buy ...?	Quero comprar ...?
Do you sell ...?	Vendem ...?
I'm just looking round	Estou somente a escolher
I don't want to buy anything now	De momento não estou interessado em nada
You'll find them in the ... department	* Encontrará isso na secção de ...
We've sold out but we'll have more tomorrow	* Não temos por agora mas amanhã já teremos
Shall we send it, or will you take it with you?	* Prefere que lhe enviemos ou leva já consigo?
Please send them to ...	Por favor, envie para ...

Choosing

What colour do you want?	* Que cor prefere?
I like this one	Gosto dêste
I prefer that one	Prefiro aquêle
I don't like the colour	Não gosto da cor
Have you a green one?	Tem um em verde?

Do you have different colours?	Tem outras cores?
Have you anything better?	Tem algo melhor?
I'd like another	Desejava outro
What size?[1]	* Que medida?
It's too big/tight	Está bastante grande/curto
Have you a larger/smaller one?	Tem um maior/mais pequeno?
What size is this?	Que medida é esta?
I want size ...	Quero número ...
The English/American size is ...	A medida inglesa/americana é ...
My collar size is ...	A minha medida de colarinho é ...
My waist measurement is ...	A minha medida de cintura é ...
My chest measurement is ...	A minha medida de peito é ...
What's it made of?	De que é feito isto?
For how long is it guaranteed?	Quanto tempo tem de garantia?

Complaints

I want to see the manager	Quero falar com o gerente
I bought this yesterday	Comprei isto ontem

1. See Table (pp. 85-86) for continental sizes.

It doesn't work | Não funciona
This is dirty/stained/torn/ broken/cracked/bad | Está sujo/manchado/roto/ estragado/partido/em más condições
Will you change it, please? | Podem trocá-lo, por favor?
Will you refund my money? | Podem devolver-me o dinheiro?

Paying

How much is this? | Quanto custa isto?
That's 500 escudos, please | * São quinhentos escudos
They are 8 escudos each | * São oito escudos cada
It's too expensive | É bastante caro
Don't you have anything cheaper? | Não tem algo mais barato?
Will you take English/ American/South African currency? | Aceitam dinheiro inglês/ americano/sul-africano?
Do you take traveller's cheques? | Aceitam cheques de viagem?
Please pay the cashier | * Pague na caixa por favor
May I have a receipt, please | Passe-me um recibo por favor
You've given me the wrong change | O troco não está certo

Clothes and shoes[1]

I want a hat/sunhat	Quero um chapéu/chapéu de sol
I'd like a pair of white cotton gloves/black leather gloves	Desejava um par de luvas brancas de algodão/negras de pele
May I see some dresses, please?	Posso ver vestidos, por favor?
I like the one in the window	Gosto do que está na montra
May I try this?	Posso provar este?
That's smart	É muito elegante
It doesn't fit me	Não me fica bem
I don't like this style	Não gosto deste modelo
Ladies'/men's coats, please	Casacos de senhora/homem, por favor
Where are beach clothes?	Onde estão roupas de praia?
Ladies' hats are on the second floor	* Os chapéus de senhora estão no segundo andar
I want a short-/long-/sleeved shirt, collar size . . .	Quero uma camisa de manga curta/larga, medida de colarinho . . .
A pair of grey wool socks, please, size . . .	Por favor, um par de meias de lã cinzenta, medida . . .

1. For sizes see pp. 85–86.

I need a pair of walking shoes/ sandals/black shoes with small heels

Quero um par de sapatos confortáveis/sandálias/sapatos negros de tacão raso

These heels are too high/too low

Este tacão é demasiado alto/ baixo

Clothing sizes

WOMEN'S DRESSES, ETC.

British	32	34	36	38	40	42	44
American	10	12	14	16	18	20	22
Continental	30	32	34	36	38	40	42

MEN'S SUITS

British and American	36	38	40	42	44	46
Continental	46	48	50	52	54	56

MEN'S SHIRTS

British and American	14	$14\frac{1}{2}$	15	$15\frac{1}{2}$	16	$16\frac{1}{2}$	17
Continental	36	37	38	39	41	42	43

STOCKINGS

British and American	8	$8\frac{1}{2}$	9	$9\frac{1}{2}$	10	$10\frac{1}{2}$	11
Continental	0	1	2	3	4	5	6

SOCKS

British and American	9½	10	10½	11	11½
Continental	38–39	39–40	40–41	41–42	42–43

SHOES

British	1	2	3	4	5	6	7	8	9	10	11	12
American	2½	3½	4½	5½	6½	7½	8½	9½	10½	11½	12½	13½
Continental	33	34–5	36	37	38	39–40	41	42	43	44	45	46

This table is only intended as a rough guide since sizes vary from manufacturer to manufacturer.

Chemist[1]

Can you prepare this prescription for me, please?	Pode aviar-me esta receita por favor?
Have you a small first-aid kit?	Tem um estojo de primeiros socorros?
A bottle of aspirin, please	Um tubo de aspirinas, por favor

1. See also AT THE DOCTOR'S (p. 108).

Can you suggest something for indigestion/constipation/diarrhoea?	Pode aconselhar-me algo para a indigestão/prisão de ventre/diarreia?
I want something for insect bites	Quero algo para picaduras de insectos
I want a mosquito repellent	Quero algo contra os mosquitos
Can you give me something for sunburn?	Tem algo para as queimaduras de sol?
I want some throat lozenges, please	Quero pastilhas para a garganta, por favor

Toilet requisites

A packet of razor blades, please	Um pacote de lâminas de barbear, por favor
How much is this after-shave lotion?	Quanto custa esta loção de barba?
A tube of toothpaste, please	Um tubo de pasta para os dentes, por favor
A box of paper handkerchiefs, please	Uma caixa de lenços de papel, por favor

I want some eau-de-cologne/[1] perfume	Um frasco de água de colónia/ perfume
May I try it?	Posso experimentar?
A shampoo for dry/greasy hair, please	Um shampoo para cabelo seco/ oleoso, por favor

Photography

I want to buy a camera	Quero comprar uma máquina fotográfica
Have you a film for this camera?	Tem rolo para esta máquina?
A 6 × 9 120 film, please	Um rolo de seis por nove cento e vinte, por favor
Give me a 35 mm. colour film with 20/36 exposures	Um rolo de cor (colorido) de trinta e cinco milímetros e de vinte/trinta e seis fotos
Would you fit the film in the camera for me, please?	Podia fazer o favor de meter o rolo na máquina?
How much is it?	Quanto é?

1. In Portugal you can buy 'loose' perfume or eau-de-cologne if you take your own bottle. This is called *perfume/água de colónia avulso*.

Does the price include processing?	A revelação está incluída no preço?
I'd like this film developed and and printed	Quero revelação e cópias deste rolo
Please enlarge this negative	Uma ampliação deste negativo, por favor
When will it be ready?	Quando estará pronto?
Will it be done tomorrow?	Estará pronto amanhã?
Will it be ready by . . .?	Pode estar pronto para . . .?
My camera's not working, can you check it/mend it?	A minha máquina não funciona podem vê-la/consertá-la?
The film is jammed	O rolo não passa

Food [1]

Give me a kilo/half a kilo of . . ., please	Um quilo (kilo)/meio quilo de . . ., por favor
100 grammes of sweets/ chocolates, please	Cem gramas de rebuçados/ bombons, por favor
A bottle/litre of milk/wine/ beer	Uma garrafa/um litro de leite/ vinho/cerveja

1. See also RESTAURANT (p. 61) and WEIGHTS AND MEASURES (p. 120).

Is there anything back on the bottle?	Devolvem algum dinheiro pela garrafa?
I want a jar/tin/packet of . . .	Quero um boião/uma lata/um pacote de . . .
Do you sell frozen foods?	Vendem alimentos congelados?
These pears are very hard	Estas peras estão muito duras
Is it fresh?	É fresco?
Are they ripe?	Estão maduros?
This is bad	É mau
A loaf of bread, please[1]	Um pão, por favor
How much a kilo/a bottle?	Quanto custa um quilo/uma garrafa?

Tobacconist[2]

Do you stock English/American/ South African cigarettes?	Tem cigarros ingleses/ americanos/sul africanos?
Virginia/dark tobacco	Tabaco amarelo/negro
What cigars have you?	Que (marcas de) charutos têm?
A packet of . . ., please	Um pacote de . . ., por favor

1. Portuguese bread: *um pão de quilo (meio quilo)* – a loaf weighing 1 kilo ($\frac{1}{2}$ kilo); *pãezinhos* – rolls; *um pão de forma* – English loaf; *pão de centeio* – rye bread; *broa* – maize bread.
2. Tobacconists often sell postage stamps.

I want some filter-tip cigarettes/ cigarettes without filter/ menthol cigarettes	Um maço de cigarros com filtro/sem filtro/mentolados
A box of matches, please	Uma caixa de fósforos, por favor
I want to buy a lighter	Quero comprar um isqueiro
Do you sell lighter fuel?	Têm gasolina para o isqueiro?
I want a gas refill for this lighter	Quero uma recarga de gás para este isqueiro

Newspapers, books, writing materials

Do you sell English/American/ South African newspapers?	Vendem jornais ingleses/ americanos/sul africanos?
Can you get . . . newspaper/ magazine for me?	Pode arranjar-me o jornal diário . . ./a revista . . .?
Where can I get the . . .?	Onde posso comprar . . .?
I want a map of the city	Quero um mapa da cidade
Is there an entertainment/ amusements guide?	Tem um programa dos espectáculos/divertimentos?
Do you have any English books?	Tem livros ingleses?
Have you any books by . . .?	Tem algum livro de . . .?
I want some colour postcards/ black and white postcards/ plain postcards	Quero postais coloridos/postais a preto e branco/postais de correio

Laundry and cleaning

I want to have these things washed/cleaned	Quero isto lavado/limpo
These stains won't come out	* Estas nódoas não se tiram
It only needs to be pressed	Só falta passar
This is torn; can you mend it?	Isto está roto; podem cosê-lo?
Do you do invisible mending?	Sabem fazer serziduras?
There's a button missing	Falta um botão
Will you sew on another one, please?	Podem pôr-me outro, por favor?
When will it be ready?	Quando estará pronto?
I need them by this evening/tomorrow	Necessito para esta noite/para amanhã
Call back at 5 o'clock	* Volte às cinco horas
We can't do it before Thursday	* Não podemos fazê-lo antes de quinta-feira
It will take three days	* Estará pronto dentro de três dias

Repairs

SHOES

I want these shoes soled with leather/heeled with rubber	Quero que me ponham meias solas de coiro nestes sapatos/saltos de borracha
Can you put on new heels?	Pode pôr saltos novos?
How much do new heels cost?	Quanto custam uns saltos novos?
Can you do them while I wait?	Pode arranjá-los já?
When should I pick them up?	Quando posso vir buscá-los?

WATCH/JEWELLERY

Can you repair this watch?	Pode reparar-me este relógio?
I need a new bracelet/strap	Eu necessito de uma pulseira/correia nova
The fastener is broken	O fecho partiu-se
The fastener won't work	O fecho estragou-se
The stone is loose	A pedra está solta
How much will it cost?	Quanto custa?
It can't be repaired	* Não tem arranjo conserto
You need a new one	* Necessita um novo/uma nova

BARBER AND HAIRDRESSER

May I make an appointment for this morning/tomorrow afternoon?	Posso marcar hora para esta manhã/para amanhã à tarde?
What time?	A que horas?
I want my hair cut/trimmed	Quero o meu cabelo cortado/aparado
Not too short at the sides	Não demasiado curto dos lados
I'll have it shorter at the back, please	Mais curto atrás, por favor
This is where I have my parting	Aqui é a risca
My hair is oily/dry	O meu cabelo é oleoso/seco
I want a shampoo	Quero que me lavem a cabeça
I want my hair washed and set	Quero que me lavem e penteem o cabelo
Please set it without rollers/on large/small rollers	Sem rolos/com rolos grandes/com rolos pequenos, por favor
I want a colour rinse	Quero uma pintura (ransagem)
I'd like to see a colour chart	Gostava de ver o catálogo das cores
I want a darker/lighter shade	Quero um tom mais escuro/mais claro
I want my hair bleached/tinted/permed	Quero fazer uma descoloração/uma pintura/uma permanente
The water is too cold	A água está demasiado fria

The dryer is too hot	O secador está demasiado quente
Thank you, I like it very much	Obrigado, está muito bem
I want a shave/manicure, please	Quero fazer a barba/manicura, por favor

POST OFFICE

Where's the main post office?	Onde é a estação principal dos correios?
Where's the nearest post office?	Onde é a estação de correios mais próxima?
What time does the post office close?	A que horas fecham os correios?
Where's the post box?	Onde há um marco de correio?

Letters and telegrams[1]

How much is a postcard to England?	Que franquia levam os postais para Inglaterra?
What's the airmail to the U.S.A.?	Que franquia levam as cartas por avião para os Estados Unidos da América?
How much is it to send a letter surface mail?	Que franquia levam as cartas por correio ordinário?
It's inland	É para Portugal
Give me three 3$50 and five 1$00 stamps, please	Três selos de três escudos e cinquenta centavos, e cinco de um escudo, por favor
I want to send this letter express	Quero mandar esta carta expresso

1. You can buy stamps from a tobacconist's, as well as from a post office.

I want to register this letter	Quero registar esta carta
Where is the poste restante section?	Onde é a secção de posta-restante?
Are there any letters for me?	Há alguma carta para mim?
What is your name?	* Qual é o seu nome?
Have you any means of identification?	* Tem algum documento de identificação?
I want to send an overnight telegram/a reply paid telegram	Quero mandar um telegrama/ um telegrama com resposta paga
How much does it cost per word?	Quanto custa por palavra?

Telephoning[1]

Where's the nearest phone box?	Onde é a cabine telefónica mais próxima?
I want to make a phone call	Quero fazer uma chamada telefónica
Please give me a token	Uma ficha, por favor
Please get me Lisbon 552379	Quero uma chamada para o 552379 de Lisboa
I want to telephone to England	Quero telefonar para Inglaterra

1. Telephone boxes are rare, but you can telephone from most cafés and bars.

I want extension 43	Quero a extensão 43
May I speak to Senhor Alves?	O senhor Alves está?/Posso falar com o senhor Alves, por favor?
Who's speaking?	Quem fala?
Hold the line, please	* Não desligue, por favor
Put the receiver down	* Desligue
He's not here	* Não está em casa/aqui
He's at . . .	* Está . . .
When will he be back?	A que horas volta?/Quando voltará?
Will you take a message?	Faz o favor de dizer-lhe . . .?
Tell him that Mr X phoned	Diga-lhe que o Senhor X telefonou
I'll ring again later	Telefonarei mais tarde
Please ask him to phone me	Por favor diga-lhe que me telefone
What's your number?	* Qual é o seu número?
My number is . . .	O meu número é . . .
I can't hear you well	Não o oiço bem
The line is engaged	* Está impedido
There's no reply	* Não respondem
You have the wrong number	* Enganou-se no número

SIGHTSEEING[1]

What ought one to see here?	O que podemos ver aqui?
What's this building?	Que edifício é este?
Where is the old part of the city?	Onde é a parte antiga da cidade?
When was it built?	Quando foi construída?
Who built it?	Quem construíu?
What's the name of this church?	Qual é o nome desta igreja?
What time is mass at church?	A que horas há missa na igreja de ...?
What time is the service?[2]	A que horas é o serviço/o culto?
Is there a protestant church/ synagogue?	Há aqui uma igreja protestante/ sinagoga?
Is this the natural history museum?	É este o museu de história natural?
When is the museum open?	A que horas está aberto o museu?
Is it open on Sundays?	Está aberto aos domingos?
The museum is closed on Mondays[3]	* O museu está fechado às segundas
Admission free	* Entrada gratuita
How much is it to go in?	Qanto custa a entrada?
Have you a ticket?	* Tem um bilhete de entrada?

1. See also BUS AND COACH TRAVEL (p. 40), DIRECTIONS (p. 43).
2. *Serviço* is a service in a Protestant church, *culto* in a Catholic church.
3. Museums are closed on Mondays and public holidays (see p. 117).

Where do I get tickets?	Onde se compram os bilhetes?
Please leave your parcels in the cloakroom	* Por favor deixem os embrulhos no guarda-roupa
It's over there	* É por ali
Can I take pictures?	Posso tirar fotografias?
Photographs are prohibited	* É proibido tirar fotografias
Follow the guide	* Siga o guia
Does the guide speak English?	O guia fala inglês?
We don't need a guide	Não precisamos de guia
Where is the . . . collection/ exhibition?	Onde é a colecção/exposição de . . .?
Where can I get a catalogue?	Onde posso obter um catálogo?
Where can I get a plan/guide book of the city?	Onde posso obter um plano/ guia da cidade?
Is this the way to the zoo?	É este o caminho para o jardim zoológico?
Which bus goes to the castle?	Que autocarro vai ao castelo?
How do I get to the park?	Como se vai para o parque?
Can we walk it?	Podemos ir a pé?

ENTERTAINMENT

What's on at the theatre/cinema?[1]	O que há de teatro/cinema?
Is there a concert?	Há algum concerto?
I want two seats for tonight	Quero dois lugares para esta noite
I want to book seats for Thursday	Quero reservar lugares para quinta-feira
Are they good seats?	São bons os lugares?
Where are these seats?	Onde são estes lugares?
What time does the performance start?	A que horas começa a sessão?
What time does it end?	A que horas termina?
A programme, please	Um programa, por favor
Which is the best nightclub?	Qual é o melhor clube nocturno?
What time is the floorshow?	A que horas é o espectáculo?
Would you like to dance?	Quere dançar?
Is there a jazz club here?	Há aqui algum clube de jazz?
Is there a discotheque here?	Há aqui discoteca?
What should one wear?	Como se deve ir vestido?

1. Cinemas usually have two or three separate performances a day. Many English and American films are shown.

SPORTS AND GAMES

Where is the stadium?	Onde é o estádio?
Are there any seats left in the grandstand?	Há alguns lugares de tribuna?
How much are the cheapest seats?	Quanto custam as entradas mais baratas?
Are the seats in the sun/shade?	Os lugares são ao sol/à sombra?
We want to go to a football match/the tennis tournament/ the bullfight	Queremos ir a um desafio de futebol, a um campeonato de tenis/a uma tourada
Who's playing?	Que equipe joga?
Who's (bull) fighting?	Quem toureia?
When does it start?	A que horas começa?
What is the score?	O que está no marcador?
Who's winning?	Quem está a ganhar?
Where's the race course?	Onde é o hipódromo?
Would you like to go hunting?	* Quer ir a uma caçada?

THE BULLFIGHT[1]	A CORRIDA DE TOUROS
The bull-ring	A praça de touros
Tickets in the sun (cheaper) in the shade (more expensive)	bilhetes de sol de sombra
Ringside (best) seats	barreiras

1. *A novilhada* is a corrida with young bulls and inexperienced bullfighters (*novilheiros*).
   In Portuguese bullfighting the bull is never killed.

Second best seats	contra-barreiras
A box	Um camarote
The balcony	A varanda
The gallery	A geral
The bullfighter	O toureiro
Horsemen with lances who weaken the bull	Os picadores
The men who place the darts in the bull's shoulder muscles	Os bandarilheiros
The darts	As bandarilhas
Red and yellow cloak used at the beginning of the corrida	A capa/o capote
Small cape used for dangerous passes	A muleta

ON THE BEACH

Which is the best beach?	Qual é a melhor praia?
Is there a quiet beach near here?	Há por aqui alguma praia sossegada?
Is it far to walk?	Pode-se ir a pé?
Is there a bus to the beach?	Há autocarro para a praia?
Is the beach sand or shingle?	É a praia de areia ou de pedras?
Is the bathing dangerous from this beach/bay?	É perigoso tomar banho nesta praia/baía?
Bathing prohibited	* Proibido tomar banho
It's dangerous	* É perigoso
Is the tide rising/falling?	Está a maré subindo/baixando?
There's a strong current here	* Há aqui muita corrente
You will be out of your depth	* Não há pé
Are you a strong swimmer?	* É bom nadador?
Is it deep?	É fundo?
Is the water cold?	Está a água fria?
It's warm	Está quente
Can one swim in the lake/river?	Pode-se nadar no lago/rio?
Is there an indoor/outdoor swimming pool?	Há piscina coberta/ao ar livre?
Is it salt or fresh water?	É água doce ou salgada?
Are there showers?	Há duches?
I want to hire a cabin for the day/morning/two hours	Quero alugar uma barraca para todo o dia/pela manhã/por duas horas

I want to hire a deckchair/ sunshade

Quero alugar uma cadeira de encosto/guarda-sol

Can we water ski here?

Pode-se fazer aqui ski aquático?

Can we hire the equipment?

Pode-se alugar o equipamento?

Where's the harbour?

Onde é o porto?

Can we go out in a fishing boat?

Pode-se saír num barco de pesca?

We want to go fishing

Queremos ir à pesca

Can I hire a rowing boat/ motor boat?

Pode-se alugar um barco a remos/um barco a motor?

What does it cost by the hour?

Quanto custa por hora?

CAMPING AND WALKING[1]

How long is the walk to the Youth Hostel?	A que distância fica o Albergue da Juventude?
How far is the next village?	A que distância fica a próxima povoação?
Is there a footpath to . . .?	Há caminho para . . .?
Is it possible to go across country?	Pode-se ir através do campo?
Is there a short cut?	Há algum atalho?
It's an hour's walk to . . .	* É uma hora de caminho a . . .
Is there a camping site near here?	Há aqui perto um parque de campismo?
Is it an authorized camp site?	É um parque autorizado?
Is drinking water/are sanitary arrangements/showers provided?	Tem água potável/instalações sanitárias/duches?
May we camp here?	Pode-se acampar aqui?
Can we hire a tent?	Podemos alugar uma tenda de campanha?
Can we park our caravan here?	Podemos estacionar aqui a nossa caravana?
Is this drinking water?	É esta água potável?
Where are the shops?	Onde são as lojas?
Where can I buy paraffin/ butane gas?	Onde posso comprar petrólio/ gas butano?

1. See also DIRECTIONS (p. 43).

| May we light a fire? | Pode-se fazer fogo? |
| Where do I dispose of rubbish? | Para onde posso atirar o lixo? |

AT THE DOCTOR'S

I must see a doctor, can you recommend one?	Preciso de ser visto por um médico, pode aconselhar-me um?
Please call a doctor	Chame um médico, por favor
I am ill	Estou doente
I've a pain in my right arm	Dói-me o braço direito
My wrist hurts	Dói-me o pulso
I think I've sprained/broken my ankle	Penso que desloquei/parti o tornozelo
I fell down and my back hurts	Caí e doem-me as costas
My foot is swollen	Tenho o pé inchado
I've burned/cut/bruised myself	Queimei-me/cortei-me/dei um golpe
My stomach is upset	Estou mal do estômago
I have indigestion	Estou com indigestão
My appetite's gone	Não tenho apetite
I think I've got food poisoning	Penso que estou intoxicado
I can't eat/sleep	Não posso comer/dormir
I am a diabetic	Sou diabético
My nose keeps bleeding	Deito sangue do nariz frequentemente
I have earache	Doem-me os ouvidos
I have difficulty in breathing	Tenho dificuldade em respirar/Não respiro bem
I feel dizzy	Estou tonto

I feel sick	Estou enjoado
I keep vomiting	Estou com vómitos
I think I've caught 'flu	Penso que estou com gripe
I've got a cold	Estou constipado/Tenho uma constipação
I've had it since yesterday/for a few hours	Tenho-a desde ontem/há algumas horas
You're hurting me	Está a magoar-me
Must I stay in bed?	Tenho que ficar na cama?
Will you call again?	Voltará?
How much do I owe you?	Quanto lhe devo?
When can I travel again?	Quando posso novamente viajar?
I feel better now	Estou melhor
Where does it hurt?	* Onde lhe dói?
Have you a pain here?	* Dói-lhe aqui?
How long have you had the pain?	* Há quanto tempo lhe dói?
Open your mouth	* Abra a boca
Put out your tongue	* Ponha a língua de fora
Breathe in	* Respire fundo
Breathe out	* Expire
Does that hurt?	* Dói-lhe?
A lot?	* Muito?
A little?	* Um pouco?

Please lie down	* Deite-se, por favor
I'll give you some pills/ medicine	* Vou dar-lhe uns comprimidos/ um remédio
Take this prescription to the chemist's	* Leve esta receita à farmácia
Take this three times a day	* Tome isto três vezes ao dia
I'll give you an injection	* Vou dar-lhe uma injecção
Roll up your sleeve	* Levante a manga
I'll put you on a diet	* Vou pô-lo a dieta
Come and see me again in two days' time	* Volte dentro de dois dias
You must be X-rayed	* Tem que tirar uma radiografia
You must go to the hospital	* Tem de ir a um hospital/a uma clínica
You must stay in bed	* Tem de ficar na cama

AT THE DENTIST'S

I must see a dentist	Tenho de ir ao dentista
Can I make an appointment	Posso fazer uma marcação?
As soon as possible	O mais depressa possível
I have toothache	Doem-me os dentes
This tooth hurts	Dói-me este dente
I've lost a filling	Caíu-me uma obturação
Can you fill it?	Pode obturar-mo?
Can you do it now?	Pode fazê-lo agora?
Will you take the tooth out?	Tem que tirar-me o dente?
Please give me an injection first	Dê-me primeiro uma injecção
My gums are swollen	Tenho as gengivas inflamadas
My gums keep bleeding	As gengivas deitam sangue
I've broken my plate, can you repair it?	Parti a dentadura, pode repará-la?
You're hurting me	Está a magoar-me
How much do I owe you?	Quanto é, por favor?/Quanto lhe devo?
When should I come again?	Quando tenho que voltar?
Please rinse your mouth	* Enxague a boca, por favor
I will X-ray your teeth	* Tenho que tirar uma radiografia aos seus dentes
You have an abscess	* Tem um abcesso
The nerve is exposed	* O nervo está exposto
This tooth can't be saved	* Este dente não se pode salvar

PROBLEMS AND ACCIDENTS

Where's the police station?	Onde é a esquadra da polícia?
Call the police	Chame a polícia
Where's the British/South African consulate?	Onde é o consulado inglês/sul africano?
Please let the consulate know	Comuniquem com o consulado, por favor
My bag has been stolen	Roubaram-me o meu saco/a minha bolsa
I found this in the street	Encontrei isto na rua
I have lost my luggage/ passport/traveller's cheques	Perdi a minha bagagem/ o meu passaporte/o meu livro de cheques
I have missed my train	Perdi o comboio
My luggage is on board	A minha bagagem está no comboio
Call a doctor	Chame um médico
Call an ambulance	Chame uma ambulância
There has been an accident	Houve um acidente
We've had an accident	Tivemos um acidente
He's badly hurt	Está gravemente ferido
He has fainted	Está desmaiado
He's losing blood	Está perdendo sangue
Please get some water/a blanket/ some bandages	Traga água/uma manta/ ligaduras, por favor
I've broken my glasses	Parti os óculos

I can't see	Não consigo ver
A child has fallen in the water	Caíu uma criança à água
A woman is drowning	Está se afogando uma mulher
May I see your insurance policy?	* Posso ver a sua apólice de seguro ?
Apply to the insurance company	* Dirija-se à companhia seguros
I want a copy of the police report	Quero uma cópia do relatório policial

TIME AND DATES

What time is it?	Que horas são?
It's one o'clock	É uma hora
2 o'clock	São duas
midday	É meio-dia
midnight	É meia-noite
quarter to ten	São dez menos um quarto
quarter past five	São cinco e um quarto
half past four	São quatro e meia
five past eight	São oito e cinco
twenty to three	São três menos vinte
twenty-five to seven	São sete menos vinte e cinco
twenty-five past eight	São oito e vinte e cinco
It's early/late	É cedo/tarde
My watch is slow/fast	O meu relógio está atrasado/ adiantado
My watch has stopped	O meu relógio parou
What time does it start/finish?	A que horas começa/termina?
Are you staying long?	Vai passar muito tempo?
I'm staying for two weeks/four days	Estarei duas semanas/quatro dias
I've been here for a week	Passei aqui uma semana
We're leaving on January 5th	Saímos a cinco de Janeiro
We got here on July 27th	Chegamos a vinte e sete de Julho

What's the date?	Que dia é hoje?
It's December 9th	É nove de Dezembro
Today	hoje
Yesterday	ontem
Tomorrow	amanhã
Day after tomorrow	depois de amanhã
Day before yesterday	anteontem
Day	dia
Morning	manhã
Afternoon	tarde
Evening	anoitecer
Night	noite
This morning	esta manhã
Yesterday afternoon	ontem à tarde
Tomorrow night	amanhã à noite
In the morning	pela manhã
In 10 days' time	dentro de dez dias
On Tuesday	na Terça-feira
On Sundays	aos Domingos
This week	esta semana
Last month	o mês passado
Next month	o próximo mês
Next year	o próximo ano

Sunday[1]	Domingo
Monday	Segunda-feira
Tuesday	Terça-feira
Wednesday	Quarta-feira
Thursday	Quinta-feira
Friday	Sexta-feira
Saturday	Sábado
January	Janeiro
February	Fevereiro
March	Março
April	Abril
May	Maio
June	Junho
July	Julho
August	Agosto
September	Setembro
October	Outubro
November	Novembro
December	Dezembro

1. In timetables the days from Monday to Friday are often abbreviated: *às 2ͣˢ*— on Mondays; *às 4ͣˢ* on Wednesdays.

PUBLIC HOLIDAYS

1 January (New Year's Day)   O dia de Ano Novo

10 June (Portuguese National Day)   O dia de Camões Portugal

Corpus Christi (Thursday of 8th week after Easter)   O dia do Corpo de Deus

15 August (The Assumption)   O dia da Assunção

5 October (Republic Day)   O dia da República

1 November (All Saints' Day)   O dia de Todos os Santos

1 December (Independence Day)   O Primeiro de Dezembro

8 December (Immaculate Conception)   O dia de Imaculada Conceicão

25 December (Christmas)   O Natal

Apart from these holidays every town and village celebrates its own holiday which usually coincides with the day of its patron saint. Although not official holidays, many businesses, shops, etc., are closed on Shrove Tuesday, Good Friday and Maundy Thursday.

NUMBERS

CARDINAL

0	zero	23	vinte e três
1	um	24	vinte e quatro
2	dois	30	trinta
3	três	31	trinta e um
4	quatro	32	trinta e dois
5	cinco	40	quarenta
6	seis	41	quarenta e um
7	sete	50	cinquenta
8	oito	60	sessenta
9	nove	70	setenta
10	dez	80	oitenta
11	onze	90	noventa
12	doze	100	cem
13	treze	101	cento e um
14	catorze	102	cento e dois
15	quinze	121	cento e vinte e um
16	dezasseis	200	duzentos
17	dezassete	300	trezentos
18	dezoito	800	oitocentos
19	dezanove	1000	mil
20	vinte	2000	dois mil
21	vinte e um	1,000,000	um milhão
22	vinte e dois		

ORDINAL

1st	primeiro, -a	half	meio, -a/metade
2nd	segundo, -a	quarter	um quarto
3rd	terceiro, -a	three-quarters	três quartos
4th	quarto, -a	a third	um terço
5th	quinto, -a	two-thirds	dois terços
6th	sexto, -a		
7th	sétimo, -a		
8th	oitavo, -a		
9th	nono, -a		
10th	décimo, -a		

WEIGHTS AND MEASURES

DISTANCE: kilometres – miles

km	miles or km	miles		km	miles or km	miles
1·6	1	0·6		14·5	9	5·6
3·2	2	1·2		16·1	10	6·2
4·8	3	1·9		32·2	20	12·4
6·4	4	2·5		40·2	25	15·3
8	5	3·1		80·5	50	31·1
9·7	6	3·7		160·9	100	62·1
11·3	7	4·4		804·7	500	310·7
12·9	8	5·0				

A rough way to convert from miles to km: divide by 5 and multiply by 8; from km to miles divide by 8 and multiply by 5.

LENGTH AND HEIGHT: centimetres – inches

cm	ins or cm	ins		cm	ins or cm	ins
2·5	1	0·4		17·8	7	2·8
5·1	2	0·8		20	8	3·2
7·6	3	1·2		22·9	9	3·5
10·2	4	1·6		25·4	10	3·9
12·7	5	2·0		50·8	20	7·9
15·2	6	2·4		127	50	19·7

A rough way to convert from inches to cm: divide by 2 and multiply by 5; from cm to inches divide by 5 and multiply by 2.

METRES – FEET

m	ft or m	ft		m	ft or m	ft
0·3	1	3·3		2·4	8	26·3
0·6	2	6·6		2·7	9	29·5
0·9	3	9·8		3	10	32·8
1·2	4	13·1		6·1	20	65·6
1·5	5	16·4		15·2	50	164
1·8	6	19·7		30·5	100	328·1
2·1	7	23				

A rough way to convert from feet to m: divide by 10 and multiply by 3; from m to ft divide by 3 and multiply by 10.

METRES – YARDS

m	yds or m	yds		m	yds or m	yds
0·9	1	1·1		7·3	8	8·8
1·8	2	2·2		8·2	9	9·8
2·7	3	3·3		9·1	10	10·9
3·7	4	4·4		18·3	20	21·9
4·6	5	5·5		45·7	50	54·7
5·5	6	6·6		91·4	100	109·4
6·4	7	7·7		457·2	500	546·8

A rough way to convert from yds to m: subtract 10 per cent from the number of yds; from m to yds add 10 per cent to the number of metres.

LIQUID MEASURES: litres – gallons

litres	galls or litres	galls	litres	galls or litres	galls
4·6	1	0·2	36·4	8	1·8
9·1	2	0·4	40·9	9	2·0
13·6	3	0·7	45·5	10	2·2
18·2	4	0·9	90·9	20	4·4
22·7	5	1·1	136·4	30	6·6
27·3	6	1·3	181·8	40	8·8
31·8	7	1·5	227·3	50	11

1 pint = 0·6 litre   1 litre = 1·8 pint

A rough way to convert from galls to litres: divide by 2 and multiply by 9; from litres to galls divide by 9 and multiply by 2.

WEIGHT: kilogrammes – pounds

kg	lb. or kg	lb.	kg	lb. or kg	lb.
0·5	1	2·2	3·2	7	15·4
0·9	2	4·4	3·6	8	17·6
1·4	3	6·6	4·1	9	19·8
1·8	4	8·8	4·5	10	22·1
2·3	5	11·0	9·1	20	44·1
2·7	6	13·2	22·7	50	110·2

A rough way to convert from lb. to kg: divide by 11 and multiply by 5; from kg to lb. divide by 5 and multiply by 11.

grammes – ounces

grammes	oz.	oz.	grammes
100	3·5	2	57·1
250	8·8	4	114·3
500	17·6	8	228·6
1,000 (1 kg)	35	16 (1 lb.)	457·2

TEMPERATURE: centigrade – fahrenheit

centigrade °C	fahrenheit °F
0	32
5	41
10	50
20	68
30	86
440	104

To convert from °F to °C: deduct 32 and multiply by $\frac{5}{9}$; from °C to °F multiply by $\frac{9}{5}$ and add 32.

VOCABULARY

A

a, an	um, uma	oo^n, ooma
able (to be)	poder	poo-**dair**
about	cerca de	**sair**-ka de
above	em cima de	e^n see ma de
abroad	estrangeiro	esh-tra^n-**zhay**-ee-roo
abscess	o abcesso	ab-**se**-soo
accept (to)	aceitar	a-say-ee-**tar**
accident	o acidente	a-see-**de**^{n}**t**
ache	a dor	dohr
acquaintance	o conhecido	koo^n-nye-**see**-doo
across	através	a-tra-**vesh**
actor	o actor	a-**tohr**
actress	a actriz	a-**treesh**
add	unir	oo-**neer**
address	a direcção	dee-re-**sow**^{n}
advice	o conselho	ko^n-**say**-llyoo
aeroplane	o avião	à-vee-**ow**^{n}
afraid (to be)	ter medo	tayr **may**-doo
after	depois	de-**poh**-eesh
afternoon	a tarde	tard
again	outra vez	**oh**-tra vaysh
age	a idade	ee-**dahd**
agency	a agência	a-**zhe**^{n}-see-a

agent	o agente	a-**zhe**n**t**
agree (to)	concordar	kon-koor-**dar**
air	o ar	ar
airbed	o colchão de ar	kohl-**show**n de ar
air-conditioning	o ar condicionado	ar kon-dee-see-oo-**nah**-doo
airline	a linha aérea	**lee**-nya a-**air**-e-a
airmail	o correio aéreo	koo-**ray**-yoo a-**air**-e-oo
airport	o aéroporto	a-air-oh-**pohr**-too
all	todo	**toh**-doo
allergy	a alergia	a-**lair**-zhee a
allow (to)	permitir	per-mee-**teer**
all right	está bem	esh-**tah** ben
almost	quase	**kwah**-ze
alone	só	so
along	ao longo	ow **lo**n-goo
already	já	zhah
alter (to)	modificar	moo-dee-fee-**kar**
although	embora	en-**bo**-ra
always	sempre	**se**n-pre
ambulance	a ambulância	an-boo-**la**n-see-a
America	os Estados Unidos	esh-**tah**-doosh oo-**nee**-doosh

American	o americano	a-me-ree-**ka**-noo
amuse	divertir	dee-ver-**teer**
amusing	divertido	dee-ver-tee-doo
anaesthetic	anestésico	a-nes-te-see-koo
ancient	antigo	a^n-**tee**-goo
and	e	ee
angry	zangado	zan-**gah**-doo
animal	o animal	a-nee-**mal**
ankle	o artelho	ar-**tay**-llyoo
annoy (to)	incomodar	ee^n-koo-moo-**dar**
another	outro	**oh**-troo
answer	a resposta	resh-**posh**-ta
answer (to)	responder	resh-po^n-**dair**
antique	antigo	a^n-**tee**-goo
any	algum	al-**goo**^{n}
anyone, someone	alguém	al-**ge**^{n}
anything, something	algo	**al**-goo
anyway	de qualquer modo	de kwal-**kair mo**-doo
anywhere, somewhere	em qualquer parte	e^n kwal-**kair** part
apartment	o apartamento	a-par-ta-**me**^{n}-too
apologize (to)	desculpar	desh-kool-**par**
appendicitis	a apendicite	a-**pe**^{n}-dee-seet
appetite	o apetite	a-pe-**teet**

apple	a maçã	ma-**sa**n
April	abril	a-**breel**
architect	o arquiteto	ar-kee-**te**-too
architecture	a arquitetura	ar-kee-te-**too**-ra
arm	o braço	**brah**-soo
around	em volta de	en **vol**-ta de
arrange	consertar	kon-ser-**tar**
arrival	a chegada	she-**gah**-da
arrive (to)	chegar	she-**gar**
art	a arte	art
art gallery	a galeria de arte	ga-le-**ree**-a dart
artist	o artista	ar-**teesh**-ta
as	como	**koh**-moo
as much as	tanto como	**tan**-too **koh**-moo
as soon as	logo que	**lo**-goo ke
as well	também	tan-**ben**
ashtray	o cinzeiro	seen-**zay**-ee-roo
ask (to)	perguntar	per-goon-**tar**
asleep	adormecido	a-door-me-**see**-doo
aspirin	a aspirina	ash-pee-**ree**-na
at	em	en
at last	por fim	poor feen
at once	em seguida	en se-**gee**-da

atmosphere	a atmosfera	at-moosh-**fair**-a
attention	a atenção	a-te^n-**sow**^{n}
August	agosto	a-**gohsh**-too
aunt	a tia	**tee**-a
Australia	Austrália	owsh-**trah**-lee-a
author	o autor	ow-**tohr**
autumn	o outono	oh-**toh**-noo
available	disponível	deesh-poo-**nee**-vel
awake	acordado	a-koor-**da**-doo
away	fora	**fo**-ra

B

baby	o, a bebé	be-be
bachelor	o solteiro	solıl-**tay**-ee-roo
back *returned*	de volta	de **vol**-ta
back	as costas	**kosh**-tash
bad	mau	mow
bag	o saco	**sa**-koo
baker's	a padaria	pa-da-**ree**-a
balcony	o balcão	bal-**kow**^{n}
ball *dance*	o baile	byl
ball *sport*	a bola	**bo**-la
ballpoint pen	o bolígrafo	boo-**lee**-gra-foo
banana	a banana	ba-**na**-na

band *music*	a orquestra	ohr-**kesh**-tra
bandage	a ligadura	lee-ga-**doo**-ra
bank	o banco	**ba**^{n}-koo
bar	o bar	bar
barber's	a barbearia	bar-bee-a-**ree**-a
basket	o cesto	**saysh**-too
bath	o banho	**ba**-nyoo
bathe (to)	banhar-se	ba-**nyar** se
bathing cap	a touca	**toh**-ka
bathing costume	o fato de banho	**fah**-too de **ba**-nyoo
bathing trunks	os calções de banho	kal-**soy**^{n}**sh** de **ba**-nyoo
bathroom	a casa de banho	**kah**-za de **ba**-nyoo
battery	a bateria	ba-te-**ree**-a
bay	a baía	ba-**ee**-a
be (to)	ser, estar	sayr, esh-**tar**
beach	a praia	**pry**-a
beard	a barba	**bar**-ba
beautiful	bonito	boo-**nee**-too
because	porque	**poor**-ke
bed	a cama	**ka**-ma
bedroom	o quarto	**kwar**-too
beef	a vaca	**vah**-ka
beer	a cerveja	ser-**vay**-zha

before	antes	antsh
begin (to)	começar	koo-me-**sar**
beginning	o começo	koo-**may**-soo
behind	atrás	a-**trash**
believe	crer	krair
bell	a campainha	ka^n-pa-**ee**-nya
belong (to)	pertencer	per-te^n-**sair**
below	em baixo	e^n by-shoo
belt	o cinto	**see**^{n}-too
berth	o beliche	be-**leesh**
best	o melhor	oo me-**lyor**
better	melhor	me-**lyor**
between	entre	**en**-tre
bicycle	a bicicleta	bee-see-**kle**-ta
big	grande	gra^{n}d
big game hunting	a caça grossa	**ka**-sa **gro**-sa
bill	a conta	**ko**^{n}-ta
bird	o pássaro	**pa**-sa-roo
birthday	o aniversário	a-nee-ver-**sah**-ree-oo
bite (to)	morder	moor-**dair**
black	negro	**nay**-groo
blanket	a manta	**ma**^{n}-ta
bleach (to)	descorar	desh-ko-**rar**

bleed (to)	sangrar	sa^n-**grar**
blister	a bolha	**bo**-llyah
blood	o sangue	sa^ng
blouse	a blusa	**bloo**-za
blue	azul	a-**zool**
(on) board	a bordo	a **bor**-doo
boarding house	a pensão	pe^n-**sow**^n
boat	o barco	**bar**-koo
body	o corpo	**kohr**-poo
bone	o osso	**oh**-soo
bone *fish*	a espinha	esh-**pee**-nyah
book	o livro	**lee**-vroo
book (to)	reservar	re-zer-**var**
booking office	a bilheteira	bee-llye-**tay**-ee-ra
bookshop	a livraria	lee-vra-**ree**-a
borrow (to)	pedir emprestado	pe-**deer** e^n-presh-**tah**-doo
both	ambos	a^n-boosh
bottle	a garrafa	ga-**rah**-fa
bottle opener	o saca-rolhas	**sa**-ka **roh**-llyash
bottom	o fundo	**foo**^n-doo
bowl	a tigela	tee-**zhe**-la
box *container*	a caixa	**ky**-sha
box *theatre*	o palco	**pal**-koo

box office	a bilheteira	bee-llye-**tay**-ee-ra
boy	o rapaz	ra-**pash**
bracelet	a pulseira	pool-**say**-ee-ra
braces	os suspensórios	soos-pe^n-**soh**-ree-osh
brain	o cérebro	se-re-broo
brake (to)	travar	tra-**var**
brandy	o conhaque	ko^n-**nyak**
brassière	o soutien	soo-tee-**a**^{n}
Brazil	o Brasil	bra-**zeel**
Brazilian	brasileiro	bra-zee-**lay**-ee-roo
bread	o pão	pow^n
break	romper	ro^n-**pair**
breakfast	o pequeno almoço	pe-**kay**-noo al-**moh**-soo
breathe (to)	respirar	resh-pee-**rar**
bridge	a ponte	po^{n}t
bright *colour*	vivo	**vee**-voo
bring (to)	trazer	tra-**zair**
British	britânico	bree-**ta**-nee-koo
broken	partido	par-**tee**-doo
brooch	o broche	brosh
brother	o irmão	eer-**mow**^{n}
brown	castanho	kash-**ta**-nyoo
bruise	a contusão	ko^n-too-**zow**^{n}

bruise (to)	contundir, pisar	koⁿ-tooⁿ-**deer**, pee-**zar**
brush	a escova	esh-**koh**-va
brush (to)	escovar	esh-koo-**var**
bucket	o balde	bald
built (to)	construir	koⁿsh-troo-**eer**
building	o edifício	e-dee-**fee**-see-oo
bullfight	a tourada	toh-**rah**-da
bullring	a praça de touros	**prah**-sa de **toh**-roosh
buoy	a boia	**boy**-a
burn (to)	queimar	kay-ee-**mar**
burst (to)	rebentar	re-beⁿ-**tar**
bus	o autocarro	ow-too-**ka**-roo
bus stop	a paragem	pa-rah-**zhe**ⁿ
business	o negócio	ne-**go**-see-oo
busy	ocupado	oh-koo-**pah**-doo
but	mas	mash
butcher's	o talho	**ta**-llyoo
butter	a manteiga	maⁿ-**tay**-ee-ga
button	o botão	boo-**tow**ⁿ
buy (to)	comprar	koⁿ-**prar**
by	por	poor

C

cabin	o camarote	ka-ma-**rot**
cable	o telegrama	te-le-**gra**-ma
café	o café	ka-**fe**
cake	o bolo	**boh**-loo
call (to) *summon, name*	chamar	sha-**mar**
(telephone) call	a chamada telefónica	sha-**mah**-da te-le-**foh**-nee-ka
call (to) *visit*	visitar	vee-zee-**tar**
camera	a máquina fotográfica	**ma**-kee-na foo-too-**gra**-fee-ka
camp (to)	acampar	a-ka^n-**par**
camp site	o acampamento	a-ka^n-pa-**me**^{n}-too
can (to be able)	poder	poo-**dair**
can *tin*	a lata	**lah**-ta
Canada	Canadá	ka-na-**dah**
Canadian	canadiano	ka-na-dee-**a**-noo
cancel (to)	anular	a-noo-**lar**
canoe	a canoa	ka-**noh**-a
cap	o gorro	**goh**-roo
capital city	a capital	ka-pee-**tal**
car	o carro	**ka**-roo
car licence	a documentação, a licença	doo-koo-me^n-ta-**sow**^{n}, lee-se^n-sa

car park	o parque de estacionamento	park desh-ta-see-oo-na-**me**^{n}-too
carafe	a garrafa	ga-**rah**-fa
caravan	a caravana	**ka**-ra-**va**-na
care	cuidado	kwee-**dah**-doo
careful	cuidadoso	kwee-da-**doh**-zoo
carry (to)	levar	le-**var**
cash (to)	trocar	troo-**kar**
cashier	o, a caixa	ky-sha
casino	o casino	ka-zee-noo
castle	o castelo	kash-**te**-loo
cat	o gato	**gah**-too
catalogue	o catálogo	ka-**ta**-loo-goo
catch (to)	apanhar	a-pa-**nyar**
cathedral	a catedral	ka-te-**dral**
catholic	católico	ka-**to**-lee-koo
cave	a caverna	ka-**vair**-na
centre	o centro	**se**^{n}-troo
century	o século	**se**-koo-loo
ceremony	a cerimónia	se-ree-**mo**-nee-a
certain	certo	**sair**-too
chair	a cadeira	ka-**day**-ee-ra
chambermaid	a criada de quarto	kree-**ah**-da de **kwar**-too

(small) change	dinheiro trocado	dee-**nyay**-ee-roo troo-**kah**-doo
change (to)	trocar	troo-**kar**
charge	a tarifa, o preço	ta-**ree**-fa, **pray**-soo
charge (to)	cobrar	koo-**brar**
cheap	barato	ba-**rah**-too
check (to)	examinar	ee-za-mee-**nar**
cheek	a face	fas
cheese	o queijo	**kay**-ee-zhoo
chemist's	a farmácia	far-**mah**-see-a
cheque	o cheque	chek
chest	o peito	**pay**-ee-too
chicken	a galinha	ga-**lee**-nya
child	a criança	kree-**a**n-sa
chill	o resfriamento	resh-**free**-u-**me**n-too
chin	o queixo	**kay**-ee-shoo
chiropodist	o pedicuro	pe-dee-**koo**-roo
chocolate	o chocolate	shoo-koo-**laht**
Christmas	o Natal	na-**tal**
church	a igreja	ee-**gray**-zha
cider	a sidra	**see**-dra
cigar	o charuto	sha-**roo**-too
cigarette	o cigarro	see-**ga**-roo
cigarette case	a cigarreira	see-ga-**ray**-ee-ra

cigarette lighter	o isqueiro	eesh-**kay**-ee-roo
cinema	o cinema	see-**nay**-ma
circle *theatre*	o anfiteatro	a^n-fee-tee-**ah**-troo
circus	o circo	**seer**-koo
city	a cidade	see-**dahd**
clean (to)	limpar	lee^n-**par**
clean	limpo	lee^n-poo
cliff	o rochedo	roo-**shay**-doo
cloakroom	o vestiário	vesh-tee-**ah**-ree-oo
clock	o relógio	re-**lo**-zhee-oo
close (to)	fechar	fe-**shar**
closed	fechado	fe-**sha**-doo
cloth	o tecido	te-**see**-doo
clothes	o vestuário	vesh-too-**ah**-ree-oo
coach *train*	a carruagem	ka-roo-**ah**-zhe^n
coach *bus*	a camioneta	ka-mee-oh-**ne**-ta
coast	a costa	**kosh**-ta
coat	o sobretudo	soh-bre-**too**-doo
coffee	o café	ka-**fe**
coin	a moeda	moo-e-da
cold	frio	**free**-oo
cold *med.*	a constipação	ko^{n}sh-tee-pa-**sow**^{n}
cold cream	o creme	krem
collar	o colarinho	koo-la-**ree**-nyoo

collar stud	o botão de colarinho	boo-**tow**ⁿ de koo-la-**ree**-nyoo
colour	a cor	kohr
colour film	o rolo colorido	roh-loo koo-loo-**ree**-doo
colour rinse	a coloração (pintura)	koo-loo-rã-**sow**ⁿ
comb	o pente	**pe**ⁿt
come (to)	vir	veer
come in	entre!	**e**ⁿ-tre
comfortable	confortável	koⁿ-foor-**tah**-vel
compartment *train*	o compartimento	koⁿ-par-tee-**me**ⁿ-too
complain (to)	queixar-se	kay-ee-**shar**-se
complete	completo	koⁿ-**ple**-too
concert	o concerto	koⁿ-**sair**-too
conductor *bus*	cobrador	koo-bra-**dohr**
conductor *orchestra*	o maestro	ma-**esh**-troo
congratulations	felicitações, parabens	fe-lee-see-ta-**soy**ⁿsh, pa-ra-**be**ⁿsh
connexion *train etc.*	ligação	lee-ga-**sow**ⁿ
constipation	a prisão de ventre	pree-**zow**ⁿ de **ve**ⁿ-tre
consul	o cônsul	**ko**ⁿ-sool
consulate	o consulado	koⁿ-soo-**lah**-doo
contain (to)	conter	koⁿ-**tair**
convenient	conveniente	koⁿ-ve-nee-**e**ⁿt

convent	o convento	ko^n-ve^n-too
conversation	a conversação	ko^n-ver-sa-sow^n
cook	o cozinheiro	koo-zee-**nyay**-ee-roo
cook (to)	cozinhar	koo-zee-**nyar**
cooked	cozinhado	koo-zee-**nya**-doo
cool	fresco	**fraysh**-koo
copper	o cobre	**ko**-bre
cork	a rolha	roh-llya
corkscrew	a saca-rolhas	**sa**-ka-**roh**-llyash
corner	o canto	**ka**^{n}-too
correct	correcto	koo-**re**-too
corridor	o corredor	koo-re-**dohr**
cosmetics	os cosméticos	koozh-**me**-tee-koosh
cost	o custo	**koosh**-too
cost (to)	custar	koosh-**tar**
cotton	o algodão	al-goo-**dow**^{n}
cotton wool	o algodão em rama	al-goo-**dow**^{n} e^n **ra**-ma
cough	a tosse	tos
count (to)	contar	ko^n-**tar**
country	o país	pa-**eesh**
countryside	o campo	**ka**^{n}-poo
course *dish*	o prato	**prah**-too
cousin	o primo	**pree**-moo

cramp	a cãibra	ky^n-bra
cream *face, etc.*	o creme	krem
cream *to eat*	a nata	**nah**-ta
cross	a cruz	kroosh
cross (to)	atravessar	a-tra-ve-**sar**
crossroads	os cruzamentos	kroo-za-me^n-toosh
cup	a chávena	**shah**-ve-na
cupboard	o armário	ar-**mah**-ree-oo
cure (to)	curar	koo-**rar**
curl (to)	frisar	free-**zar**
current	a corrente	koo-**re**^{n}t
curtain	a cortina	kor-**tee**-na
custard	a nata	**nah**-ta
customs	a alfândega	al-**fa**^{n}-de-ga
customs officer	o funcionário aduaneiro	foo^n-see-oo-**nah**-ree-oo a-doo-a-**nay**-ce-roo
cut (to)	cortar	koor-**tar**

D

daily	diário	dee-**ah**-ree-oo
damaged	danificado	da-nee-fee-**ka**-doo
damp	húmido	**oo**-mee-doo
dance	a dança	**da**^{n}-sa
dance (to)	dançar	da^n-**sar**

danger	o perigo	pe-**ree**-goo
dangerous	perigoso	pe-ree-**goh**-zoo
dark	escuro	esh-**koo**-roo
date	a data	**da**-ta
daughter	a filha	**fee**-llya
day	o dia	**dee**-a
dead	morto	**mohr**-too
deaf	surdo	**soor**-doo
dear	querido, caro	ke-**ree**-doo, **kah**-roo
December	dezembro	de-ze^n-broo
deck	a coberta	koo-**bair**-ta
deckchair	a cadeira de praia	ka-**day**-ee-ra de **pry**-a
declare (to)	declarar	de-kla-**rar**
deep	profundo	proo-**foo**^{n}-doo
delay	o atraso	a-**trah**-zoo
delicatessen	a mercearia	mer-see-a-**ree**-a
deliver (to)	entregar	e^n-tre-**gar**
delivery	a entrega	e^n-**tre**-ga
demi-pension	meia pensão	**may**-ya pe^n-**sow**^{n}
dentist	a dentista	de^n-**teesh**-ta
deodorant	o desodorizante	de-zoh-doo-ree-**za**^{n}t
depart (to)	partir	par-**teer**
department	o departamento	de-par-ta-**me**^{n}-too

department store	o armazém	ar-ma-**zay**^{n}
departure	a partida	par-**tee**-da
dessert	a sobremesa	soh-bre-**may**-za
detour	o desvio	dezh-**vee**-oo
develop (film)	revelar	re-ve-**lar**
diabetic	diabético	dee-a-**be**-tee-koo
diamond	o diamante	dee-a-**ma**^{n}**t**
diarrhoea	a diarreia	dee-a-**re**-ya
dictionary	o dicionário	dee-see-oo-**nah**-ree-oo
diet	a dieta	dee-e-ta
diet (to)	fazer dieta	fa-**zair** dee-e-ta
different	diferente	dee-fe-**re**^{n}**t**
difficult	difícil	dee-**fee**-seel
dine (to)	jantar	zha^n-**tar**
dining room	a sala de jantar	**sa**-la de zha^n-**tar**
dinner	o jantar	zha^n-**tar**
direction	a direcção	dee-re-**sow**^{n}
dirty	sujo	**soo**-zhoo
discothèque	a discoteca	deesh-koo-te-ka
dish	o prato	**prah**-too
disinfectant	o desinfectante	de-see^n-fek-**ta**^{n}**t**
distance	a distância	deesh-**ta**^{n}-see-a
disturb (to)	perturbar	per-toor-**bar**

dive (to)	mergulhar	mer-goo-llyar
diving board	o trampolim	tra^n-poo-**lee**^{n}
divorced	divorciado	dee-voor-see-**ah**-doo
dizzy	estonteado	esh-to^n-tee-**ah**-doo
do (to)	fazer	fa-**zair**
dock (to)	atracar	a-tra-**kar**
doctor	o médico	**me**-dee-koo
dog	o cão	kow^n
doll	a boneca	boo-**ne**-ka
dollar	o dolar	**do**-lar
door	a porta	**por**-ta
double	dobro	**doh**-broo
double bed	a cama de casal	**ka**-ma de ka-**zal**
double room	o quarto de casal	**kwar**-too de ka-**zal**
down (stairs)	abaixo	a-**by**-shoo
dozen	a dúzia	**doo**-zee-a
drawer	a gaveta	ga-**vay**-ta
dress	o vestido	vesh-**tee**-doo
dressing gown	o roupão	roh-**pow**^{n}
dressmaker	a modista	moo-**deesh**-ta
drink (to)	beber	be-**bair**
drinking water	a água potável	**a**-gwa poo-**tah**-vel
drive (to)	conduzir, guiar	ko^n-doo-**zeer**, gee-**ar**

driver	o condutor	ko^n-doo-**tohr**
driving licence	a carta de condução	**kar**-ta de ko^n-doo-**sow**^{n}
dry (to)	secar	se-**kar**
dry cleaning	a limpeza a seco	lee^n-**pay**-za a **say**-koo
duck	o pato	**pa**-too
during	durante	doo-**ra**^{n}**t**

E

each	cada	**ka**-da
ear	o ouvido	oh-**vee**-doo
earache	a dor de ouvidos	dohr doh-**vee**-doosh
early	matutino	ma-too-**tee**-noo
earrings	brincos	**bree**^{n}-koosh
east	este	esht
Easter	a Páscoa	**pash**-kwa
easy	fácil	**fah**-seel
eat (to)	comer	koo-**mair**
egg	o ovo	**oh**-voo
elastic	o elástico	ee-**lash**-tee-koo
elbow	o cotovelo	koo-too-**vay**-loo
electric light bulb	a lâmpada	**la**^{n}-pa-da
elevator	o elevador	ee-le-va-**dohr**
embassy	a embaixada	e^n-by-**shah**-da

P.P.B.—6

emergency exit	saída de emergência	sa-**ee**-da de ee-mer-**zhen**-see-a
empty	vazio	va-**zee**-oo
end	o fim	fee^n
engine	a máquina	**ma**-kee-na
England	a Inglaterra	ee^n-gla-**te**-ra
English	inglês	ee^n-**glaysh**
enlargement	a ampliação	a^n-plee-a-**sow**^{n}
enough	bastante	bash-**ta**^{n}**t**
enquires	a informação	ee^n-foor-ma-**sow**^{n}
entrance	a entrada	e^n-**trah**-da
envelope	o envelope	e^n-ve-**lop**
equipment	o equipamento	ee-kee-pa-**me**^{n}-too
Europe	a Europa	ay-oo-**ro**-pa
evening	a noite	**noh**-eet
every	cada	**ka**-da
everybody	todos	**toh**-doosh
everything	tudo	**too**-doo
everywhere	em toda a parte	e^n **toh**-da part
example	o exemplo	ee-**ze**^{n}-ploo
except	excepto	esh-**se**-too
excess	o excesso	esh-**se**-soo
exchange bureau	a casa de câmbio	**kah**-za de **ka**^{n}-bee-oo
exchange rate	o câmbio	**ka**^{n}-bee-oo

excursion	a excursão	esh-koor-**sow**ⁿ
exhibition	a exposição	esh-poo-zee-**sow**ⁿ
exit	a saída	sa-**ee**-da
expect (to)	esperar	esh-pe-**rar**
expensive	caro	**kah**-roo
express	expresso	esh-**pre**-soo
express train	o rápido	**ra**-pee-doo
eye	o olho	**oh**-llyoo
eye shadow	o rimel	ree-**mel**

F

face	a cara, o rosto	**kah**-ra, **rohsh**-too
face cream	o creme de rosto	krem de **rohsh**-too
face powder	o pó de arroz	po da-**rohsh**
factory	a fábrica	**fa**-bree-ka
faint (to)	desmaiar	dezh-my-**yar**
fair *fête*	a feira	**fay** ee-ra
fair *blonde*	loiro	**loh**-ee-roo
false teeth	os dentes postiços	**de**ⁿ-tesh poosh-tee-**soosh**
fall (to)	cair	ka-**eer**
family	a família	fa-**mee**-lee-a
far	longe	**lo**ⁿzh
fare	o bilhete	bee-**llyayt**

farm	a quinta	**kee**^{n}-ta
farther	mais longe	mysh lo^{n}zh
fashion	a moda	**mo**-da
fast	rápido	**ra**-pee-doo
fat	gordo	**gohr**-doo
father	o pai	py
fault	a culpa	**kool**-pa
February	fevereiro	fe-**vray**-ee-roo
feel (to)	sentir	se^n-**teer**
fetch (to)	buscar	boosh-**kar**
fever	a febre	**fe**-bre
few	pouco	**poh**-koo
field	o campo	**ka**^{n}-poo
fig	o figo	**fee**-goo
fill (to)	encher	e^n-**shayr**
filling *tooth*	obturação	ohb-too-ra-sow^n
film *for camera*	o rolo, a película	**roh**-loo, pe-**lee**-koo-la
film *cinema*	a película, o filme	pe-**lee**-koo-la, feelm
find (to)	encontrar	e^n-ko^n-**trar**
fine	a multa	**mool**-ta
finger	o dedo	**day**-doo
finish (to)	acabar	a-ka-**bar**
finished	acabado	a-ka-**bah**-doo

fire	o fogo	**foh**-goo
first	primeiro	pree-**may**-ee-roo
first class	primeira classe	pree-**may**-ee-ra klas
fish	o peixe	**pay**-eesh
fish (to)	pescar	pesh-**kar**
fisherman	o pescador	pesh-ka-**dohr**
fishmonger's	a peixaria	pay-sha-**ree**-a
fit (to)	sentar	se^n-**tar**
flag	a bandeira	ba^n-**day**-ee-ra
flat *level*	plano	**pla**-noo
flat	o apartamento	a-par-ta-**me**^{n}-too
flight	o vôo	**voh**-oo
flint *lighter*	a pedra	**pe**-dra
flood	a inundação	ee-noo^n-da-**sow**^{n}
floor	o chão	**show**^{n}
floor *storey*	o andar	a^n-**dahr**
floor show	o espectáculo	esh-pe-ta-**koo**-loo
florist's	a florista	floo-**reesh**-ta
flower	a flor	flohr
fly	a mosca	**mohsh**-ka
fly (to)	voar	voo-**ar**
follow (to)	seguir	se-**geer**
food	a comida	koo-**mee**-da

food poisoning	a intoxicação	een-tok-see-ka-sown
foot	o pé	pe
football	o futebol	**foot**-bol
footpath	o caminho	ka-**mee**-nyoo
for	por, para	poor, **pa**-ra
forehead	a testa	**tesh**-ta
forest	a floresta	floo-**resh**-ta
forget (to)	esquecer	esh-ke-**sair**
fork	o garfo	**gar**-foo
forward	adiante	a-dee-**ant**
fracture	a fractura	frak-**too**-ra
fragile	frágil	**frah**-zheel
France	a França	**fran**-sa
free	livre	**lee**-vre
French	francês	fran-**saysh**
fresh	fresco	**fraysh**-koo
fresh water	a água fresca	a-gwa **fraysh**-ka
Friday	sexta-feira	**saysh**-ta **fay**-ee-ra
fried	frito	**free**-too
friend	o amigo	a-**mee**-goo
from	de	de
(in) front	frente	**frent**
frontier	a fronteira	fron-**tay**-ee-ra

frozen	congelado	ko^n-zhe-**lah**-doo
fruit	a fruta	**froo**-ta
fruiterer's	a frutaria	froo-ta-**ree**-a
fruit juice	o sumo de frutas	**soo**-moo de **froo**-tash
full	cheio	**shay**-yoo
full board	pensão completa	pe^n-**sow**^{n} ko^n-**ple**-too
funny	engraçado	e^n-gra-**sah**-doo
fur	a pele	pel

G

gallery	a galeria	ga-le-**ree**-a
gamble (to)	jogar	zhoo-**gar**
game	o jogo	**zhoh**-goo
game reserve	a reserva de caça	re-**zair**-va de **ka**-sa
garage	a garagem	ga-**rah**-zhe^n
garden	o jardim	zhar-**dee**^{n}
garlic	o alho	**a**-llyoo
gate	a entrada	e^n-**trah**-da
gentleman	cavalheiro, senhor	ka vn **llycy-ec-roo**, se-**nyohr**
gentlemen	os cavalheiros	ka-va-**llyay** ee-roosh
German	alemão	a-le-**mow**^{n}
Germany	a Alemanha	a-le-**ma**-nya

get (to)	obter	ohb-**tair**
get off (to)	sair	sa-**eer**
get on (to)	montar em	mo^n-**tar**-e^n
gift	o presente	pre-ze^{n}t
girdle	a cinta	**see**^{n}-ta
girl	a rapariga	ra-pa-**ree**-ga
give (to)	dar	dar
glad	contente	ko^n-**te**^{n}t
glass	o copo	**ko**-poo
glasses	os óculos	**o**-koo-loosh
gloves	as luvas	**loo**-vash
go (to)	ir	eer
God	Deus	**day**-oosh
gold	o ouro	**oh**-roo
good	bom	bo^n
good afternoon, evening	boa tarde boa noite	**boh**-a tard **boh**-a-**noh**-eet
good-bye	adeus	a-**day**-oosh
good day, morning	bom dia	bo^n **dee**-a
good night	boa noite	**boh**-a **noh**-eet
government	o governo	goo-**vair**-noo
granddaughter	a neta	**ne**-ta
grandfather	o avô	a-**voh**
grandmother	a avó	a-**voo**

grandson	o neto	**ne**-too
grape	a uva	**oo**-va
grapefruit	a toranja	toor-a^n-zha
grass	a relva	**rel**-va
grateful	agradecido	a-gra-de-**see**-doo
great	grande	gra^{n}d
green	verde	vayrd
greengrocer's	loja de hortaliça	lo-zha de ohr-ta-**lee**-sa
grey	cinzento	see^n-**ze**^{n}-too
grocer's	a mercearia	mer-see-a-**ree**-a
groceries	os artigos de mercearia	ar-**tee**-goosh de mcr-scc-a-**ree**-a
guarantee	o garantia	ga-ra^n-**tee**-a
guest	o hóspede	**osh**-ped
guide	o guia	**gee**-a
guide book	o guia	**gee**-a
gum	a gengiva	zhe^n-**zhee**-va

H

hair	o cabelo	ka-**bay**-loo
hair brush	a escova de cabelo	esh-**koh**-va de ka-**bay**-loo
haircut	o corte de cabelo	kort de ka-**bay**-loo
hairdresser's *ladies'*	o cabeleireiro	ka-be-lay-**ray**-ee-roo

hairdresser's *men's*	o barbeiro	bar-**bay**-ee-roo
hairgrips, hairpins	os ganchos	**ga**n-shoosh
half	metade	me-**tahd**
half fare	meio bilhete	**may**-yoo bee-**llyayt**
ham	o presunto	pre-**zoo**n-too
hand	a mão	mown
handbag	a carteira	kar-**tay**-ee-ra
handkerchief	o lenço	**le**n-soo
hanger	o cabide	ka-**beed**
happen (to)	acontecer	a-kon-te-**sair**
happy	feliz	fe-**leesh**
harbour	o porto	**pohr**-too
hard *difficult*	difícil	dee-**fee**-seel
hat	o chapéu	sha-**pe**-oo
have (to)	ter	tair
have to (to)	ter obrigação de	tair oh-bree-ga-**sow**n de
hay-fever	a febre dos fenos	**fe**-bre doosh **fay**-noosh
he	ele	**ee**-le
head	a cabeça	ka-**bay**-sa
headache	a dor de cabeça	dohr de ka-**bay**-sa
head waiter	o chefe de mesa	shef de **may**-za
health	a saúde	sa-**ood**

hear (to)	ouvir	oh-**veer**
heart	o coração	koo-ra-**sow**[n]
heat	o calor	ka-**lohr**
heating	o aquecimento	a-ke-see-**me**[n]-too
heavy	pesado	pe-zah-doo
heel *foot*	o calcanhar	kal-ka-**nyar**
heel *shoe*	o tacão	ta-**kow**[n]
help	a ajuda	a-**zhoo**-da
help (to)	ajudar	a-zhoo-**dar**
her, hers	seu *m*, sua *f*	**se**-oo, **soo**-a
here	aqui	a-**kee**
high	alto	**al**-too
hill	a colina	koo-**lee**-na
hip	a anca	a[n]-ka
hire (to)	alugar	a-loo-**gar**
his	seu *m*, sua *f*	**se**-oo, **soo**-a
hitch hike (to)	pedir boleia	pe-**deer** boo-**le**-ya
holiday	o feriado	fe-ree-**ah**-doo
holidays	as férias	**fe**-ree-ash
(at) home	em casa	e[n] **kah**-za
honey	o mel	mel
hors d'œuvre	o hors d'œuvre	or **der**-vre
horse	o cavalo	ka-**vah**-loo

hospital	o hospital	ohsh-pee-**tal**
hot	quente	ke^{n}t
hotel	o hotel	oh-**tel**
hotel keeper, manager	o gerente	zhe-**re**^{n}t
hot water bottle	a botija	boo-**tee**-zha
hour	a hora	**o**-ra
house	a casa	**kah**-za
how?	como?	**koh**-moo
how much, many?	quantos?	**kwa**^{n}-toosh
hungry	fome	fom
hunt (to) *game*	caçar	**ka**-sar
hurry (to)	ter pressa	tair **pre**-sa
hurt (to)	doer	doo-**air**
husband	o marido	ma-**ree**-doo

I

I	eu	ay-oo
ice	o gelo	**zhay**-loo
ice cream	o gelado	zhe-**lah**-doo
if	se	se
ill	doente	doo-**e**^{n}t
illness	a doença	doo-**e**^{n}-sa
immediately	imediatamente	ee-me-dee-ah-ta-**me**^{n}t

important	importante	ee^n-poor-**ta**^{n}t
in	dentro	**de**^{n}-troo
include	incluir	ee^n-kloo-**eer**
included	incluido	ee^n-kloo-ee-doo
inconvenient	incómodo	ee^n-**ko**-moo-doo
incorrect	incorrecto	ee^n-koo-re-too
indigestion	a indigestão	ee^n-dee-zhesh-**tow**^{n}
infection	a infecção	ee^n-fe-**sow**^{n}
influenza	a gripe	greep
information	a informação	ee^n-foor-ma-**sow**^{n}
injection	a injecção	ee^n-zhe-**sow**^{n}
ink	a tinta	**tee**^{n}-ta
inn	a pensão, o albergue	pe^n-**sow**^{n}, al-**berg**
insect	o insecto	ee^n-**sek**-too
insect bite	a picadura de insecto	pee-**kah**-doo-ra de ee^n-**sek**-too
inside	dentro (de)	**de**^{n}-troo (de)
insomnia	a insónia	ee^n-**so**-nee-a
insurance	o seguro	se-**goo**-roo
insure (to)	segurar	se-goo-**rar**
interesting	interessante	ee^n-te-re-**sa**^{n}t
interpreter	intérprete	ee^n-**tair**-pret
into	dentro, em	**de**^{n}-troo, e^n

introduce	introduzir	een-troo-doo-**zeer**
invitation	o convite	kon-**veet**
invite (to)	convidar	kon-vee-**dar**
Ireland	a Irlanda	eer-lan-da
Irish	irlandês	eer-lan-**daysh**
iron (to)	passar a ferro	pa sar a fe roo
island	a ilha	ee-llya
it	ele *m*, ela *f*	ayl, e-la
Italian	italiano	ee-ta-lee-**a**-noo
Italy	a Itália	ee-**tah**-lee-a

J

jacket	o casaco	ka-**zah**-koo
jam	a compota	kon-**po**-ta
January	janeiro	zha-**nay**-ee-roo
jar	o jarro	**zha**-roo
jaw	a mandíbula	man-**dee**-boo-la
jellyfish	a acalefa	a-ka-**lay**-fa
jeweller's	o joalheiro	zho-a-**llyay**-roo
jewellery	a joalharia, as jóias	zho-a-llya-**ree**-a, **zhoy**-ash
journey	a viagem	vee-**ah**-zhen
jug	a jarra	**zha**-ra
juice	o sumo	**soo**-moo

July	Julho	**zhoo**-llyoo
June	Junho	**zhoo**-nyoo
jumper	a blusa	**bloo**-za

K

keep (to)	guardar	gwar-**dar**
key	a chave	shahv
kidney	o rim	ree^n
kind	o género	**zhe**-ne-roo
king	o rei	**ray**-ee
kitchen	a cozinha	koo-**zee**-nya
knee	o joelho	zhoo-**ay**-llyoo
knickers, briefs	as calcinhas	kal-**see**-nyash
knife	a faca	**fah**-ka
know (to) *fact*	saber	sa-**bair**
know (to) *person*	conhecer	koo-nyc-**sair**

L

label	a etiqucta	ee-tee-**kay**-ta
lace	a renda	**re**^{n}-da
ladies	as senhoras	se-**nyoh**-rash
lamb	o cordeiro	koor-**day**-ee-roo
lamp	a lâmpada	**la**^{n}-pa-da
landlord	o proprietário	proo-pree-e-**ta**-ree-oo

lane	o caminho	ka-**mee**-nyoo
language	a língua, o idioma	lee^n-gwa, ee-dee-**oh**-ma
large	grande	gra^nd
last	último	**ool**-tee-moo
late	tarde	tard
laugh (to)	rir	reer
laundry	a lavandaria	la-va^n-da-**ree**-a
lavatory	a retrete	re-**trayt**
lavatory paper	o papel higiénico	pa-**pel** ee-zhee-e-nee-koo
law	a lei	le-ee
laxative	o laxativo	lak-sa-**tee**-voo
lead (to)	conduzir	ko^n-doo-**zeer**
learn (to)	aprender	a-pre^n-**dair**
leather	o couro, o cabedal	**koh**-oo-roo, ka-be-**dal**
leave (to) *abandon*	deixar	day-ee-**shar**
leave (to) *go out*	sair	sa-**eer**
left *opp. right*	esquerdo	esh-**kayr**-doo
left luggage	o depósito de bagagem	de-**po**-zee-too de ba-**gah**-zhe^n
leg	a perna	**pair**-na
lemon	o limão	lee-**mow**^n
lemonade	a limonada	lee-moo-**nah**-da

lend (to)	emprestar	eⁿ-presh-**tar**
less	menos	**me**-noosh
let (to)	arrendar	a-reⁿ-**dar**
let *allow*	consentir	koⁿ-seⁿ-**teer**
letter	a carta	**kar**-ta
lettuce	a alface	al-**fas**
library	a biblioteca	bee-blee-oo-te-ka
licence	a licença	lee-seⁿ-sa
life	a vida	**vee**-da
lift	o elevador	ee-le-va-**dohr**
light *colour*	claro	**klah**-roo
light	a luz	loosh
light meter	o fotómetro	foo-**to**-mee-troo
lighter	o isqueiro	eesh-**kay**-ee-roo
lighter fuel	a gasolina/benzina	ga-zoo-**lee**-na/ ben-**zee**-na
lighthouse	o farol	fa-**rol**
like (to)	gostar	goosh-**tar**
linen	o linho	**lee**-nyoo
lip	o lábio	**lah**-bee-oo
lipstick	o baton	**ba**-toⁿ
listen	cscutar	esh-koo-**tar**
little	pouco	poh-koo
live (to)	viver	vee-**vair**

liver	o fígado	**fee**-ga-doo
loaf	o pão	pow^n
local	local	loo-**kal**
lock (to)	fechar à chave	fe-**shar** ah shahv
long	longo	**lo**^{n}-goo
look (to)	olhar	oh-**llyar**
look (to) *seem*	parecer	pa-re-**sair**
look for (to)	procurar	proo-koo-**rar**
lorry	a caminheta	ka-mee-**nye**-ta
lose (to)	perder	pair-**dair**
lost property office	secção de objectos perdidos	sek-**sow**^{n} de ob-**zhe**-toosh pair-**dee**-doosh
loud	ruidoso	roo-ee-**doh**-zoo
love (to)	amar	a-**mar**
lovely	formoso	foor-**moh**-zoo
low	baixo	**by**-shoo
luggage	a bagagem	ba-**gah**-zhe^n
lung	o pulmão	pool-**mow**^{n}
M		
magazine	a revista	re-**veesh**-ta
maid	a moça	**moh**-sa
mail	o correio	koo-**ray**-yoo

main street	a rua principal	roo-a preen-see-**pal**
make (to)	fazer	fa-**zair**
make-up	a maquilhagem	ma-kee-**llyah**-zhen
man	o homem	o-men
manager	o director, gerente	dee-re-**tohr**, zhe-**rent**
manicure	a manicura	ma-nee-**koo**-ra
many	muitos	**mwee**-toosh
map	o mapa	**ma**-pa
March	março	**mar**-soo
market	o mercado	mer-**kah**-doo
marmalade	a marmelada	mar-me-**lah**-da
married	casado	ka-**zah**-doo
Mass	a missa	**mee**-sa
match	o fósforo	**fosh**-foo-roo
match *sport*	o desafio	de-za-**fee**-oo
material	o material	ma-te-ree-**al**
mattress	o colchão	kohl-**shown**
May	maio	**my**-oo
meal	a refeição	re-fay-ee-**sown**
measurements	os medidas	me-**dee**-dash
meat	a carne	karn
medicine	o medicamento	me-dee-ka-**men**-too
meet (to)	encontrar	en-kon-**trar**

melon	o melão	me-**low**^{n}
mend (to)	reparar	re-pa-**rar**
menu	a ementa	ee-**me**^{n}-ta
message	o recado	re-**kah**-doo
metal	o metal	me-**tal**
midday	o meio-dia	**may**-yoo **dee**-a
middle	médio	**me**-dee-oo
midnight	a meia-noite	**may**-ya **noh**-eet
milk	o leite	**lay**-eet
mineral water	a água mineral	**a**-gwa mee-ne-**ral**
minute	o minuto	mee-**noo**-too
mirror	o espelho	esh-**pe**-llyoo
Miss	menina	me-**nee**-na
miss (to) *train, etc.*	perder	pair-**dair**
mistake	o erro	**ay**-roo
modern	o moderno	moo-**dair**-noo
moment	o momento	moo-**me**^{n}-too
monastery	o mosteiro, o convento	moosh-**tay**-ee-ro, ko^n-**ve**^{n}-too
Monday	segunda-feira	se-goo^n-da **fay**-ee-ra
money	o dinheiro	dee-**nyay**-ee-roo
money order	o vale postal	val poosh-**tal**
month	o mês	maysh
monument	o monumento	moo-noo-**me**^{n}-too

more	mais	mysh
morning	a manhã	ma-**nya**^{n}
mosquito	o mosquito	moosh-**kee**-too
mother	a mãe	my^n
motor	o motor	moh-**tohr**
motor boat	o barco a motor	**bar**-koo a moh-**tohr**
motor cycle	o motocicleta	mo-toh-see-**kle**-ta
motor racing	a corrida de automóveis	koo-**ree**-da de ow-too-**mo**-vaysh
motorway	a auto-estrada	**ow**-too esh-**trah**-da
mountain	a montanha	**mo**^{n}ta-nya
mouth	a boca	**boh**-ka
Mr	o senhor	se-**nyhor**
Mrs	a senhora	se-**nyoh**-ra
much	muito	**mwee**-too
muscle	o músculo	**moosh**-koo-loo
museum	o museu	moo-**zay**-oo
mushroom	o cogumelo	koo-goo-**me**-loo
music	a música	**moo**-zee-ka
must (to have to)	dever	de-**vair**
mustard	a mostarda	moosh-**tar**-da
mutton	o carnciro	kar-**nay**-ee-roo
my, mine	meu *m*, minha *f*	**me**-oo, mee-nya

N

nail *finger*	a unha	**oo**-nya
nailbrush	a escôva de unhas	esh-**koh**-va de **oo**-nyash
nailfile	a lima	**lee**-ma
name	o nome	nohm
napkin	o guardanapo	gwar-da-**na**-poo
nappy	a fralda	**fral**-da
narrow	estreito	esh-**tray**-ee-too
nausea	a náusea	**now**-zee-a
near	perto	**pair**-too
necessary	necessário	ne-se-**sah**-ree-oo
neck	o pescoço	pesh-**koh**-soo
necklace	o colar	koo-**lar**
need (to)	necessitar	ne-ce-see-**tar**
needle	a agulha	a-**goo**-lya
nerve	o nervo	**nair**-voo
never	nunca	**noo**^{n}-ka
new	novo	**noh**-voo
news	as notícias	noo-**tee**-see-ash
newsagent	a tabacaria	ta-ba-ka-**ree**-a
newspaper	o jornal	zhoor-**nal**
next	próximo	**pro**-see-moo
nice	bonito	boo-**nee**-too

night	a noite	**noh**-eet
nightclub	o clube nocturno	kloob no-**toor**-noo
nightdress	a camisa de noite	ka-**mee**-za de **noh**-eet
no	não	now^n
nobody	ninguém	nee^n-ge^n
noisy	ruidoso	roo-ee-**doh**-zoo
none	nenhum	ne-**nyoo**^{n}
north	o norte	nort
nose	o nariz	na-**reesh**
not	não	now^n
note *money*	a nota	**no**-ta
notebook	o livro de notas	**lee**-vroo de **no**-tash
nothing	nada	**nah**-da
notice	o aviso	a-vee-zoo
novel	o romance, a novela	roo-**ma**^{n}s, noo-**ve**-la
November	novembro	noo-**ve**^{n}-broo
number	o número	**noo**-me-roo
nurse	a enfermeira	en-fer-**may**-ee-ra
nut	a nóz	nosh
nylon	o nylon	**ny**-lo^n

O

occupied	ocupado	oh-koo-**pah**-doo
October	outubro	oh-**too**-broo
odd *strange*	raro	**rah**-roo
of	de	de
office	o escritório	esh-kree-**to**-ree-oo
often	muitas vezes	**mwee**-tash **vay**-zesh
oil	o azeite	a-**zay**-eet
oily	oleoso	oh-lee-**oh**-zoo
ointment	a pomada	poo-**mah**-da
old	velho	**ve**-lyoo
olive	a azeitona	a-zay-ee-**toh**-na
on	em	e^n
once	uma vez	**oo**-ma vaysh
only	somente	so-**me**^{n}t
open (to)	abrir	a-**breer**
open *p.p*	aberto	a-**bair**-too
opera	a ópera	**o**-pe-ra
operation	a operação	oh-pe-ra-**sow**^{n}
opposite	oposto	oh-**pohsh**-too
optician	o oculista	oh-koo-**leesh**-ta
or	ou	oh
orange	a laranja	la-**ra**^{n}-zha

orchestra	a orquestra	ohr-**kesh**-tra
order (to)	encomendar	e^n-koo-me^n-**dar**
ordinary	vulgar	vool-**gar**
other	outro	**oh**-troo
our, ours	nosso *m*, nossa *f*	**no**-so, **no**-sa
out, outside	fora	**fo**-ra
over	sôbre	**soh**-bre
overcoat	o sobretudo	soh-bre-**too**-doo
over there	ali	a-**lee**
owe (to)	dever	de-**vair**
owner	o proprietário	proo-pree-e-**tah**-ree-o

P

packet	o pacote	pa-**kot**
page	a página	**pa**-zhee-na
paid	pago	**pah**-goo
pain	a dôr	dohr
paint (to)	pintar	pee^n-**tar**
painting	a pintura	pee^n-**too**-ra
pair	o par	pahr
palace	o palácio	pa-**la**-see-oo
pale	pálido	**pa**-lee-doo
paper	o papel	pa-**pel**
paraffin	o petróleo	pe-**tro**-lee-oo

parcel	o pacote	pa-**kot**
park (to)	estacionar	esh-ta-see-oo-**nar**
park	o parque	park
part	a parte	part
parting *hair*	a risca	**reesh**-ka
pass (to)	passar	pa-**sar**
passenger	o passageiro	pa-sa-**zhay**-ee-roo
passport	o passaporte	pa-sa-**port**
path	o caminho	ka-**mee**-nyoo
patient	o doente	doo-e^{n}t
pavement	o passeio	pa-**say**-yoo
pay (to)	pagar	pa-**gar**
pea	a ervilha	er-**vee**-lya
peach	o pêssego	**pe**-se-goo
pear	a pêra	**pe**-ra
pebble	o seixo	**se**-ee-shoo
pedestrian	o peão	pee-**ow**^{n}
pen	a pena	**pe**-na
pencil	o lápis	**lah**-pesh
penknife	o canivete	ka-nee-**vet**
people	a gente	zhe^{n}t
pepper	a pimenta	pee-**me**^{n}-ta
performance	o espectáculo	es-pe-**ta**-koo-loo

perfume	o perfume	pcr-**foom**
perhaps	talvez	tal-**vaysh**
perm	a permanente	per-ma-**ne**ⁿt
permit	a autorização	ow-too-ree-za-**sow**ⁿ
permit (to)	permitir	per-mee-**teer**
person	a pessoa	pe-**soh**-a
personal	pessoal	pe-soo-**al**
petrol	a gazolina	ga-zoo-**lee**-na
petrol can	a lata de gazolina	**lah**-ta de ga-zoo-**lee**-na
petrol station	a estação de serviço	esh-ta-**sow**ⁿ de ser-**vee**-soo
photograph	a fotografia	foo-too-gra-**fee**-a
photographer	a fotógrafo	foo-**to**-gra-foo
piano	o piano	pee-**a**-noo
picnic	a merenda	me-**re**ⁿ-da
picnic (to)	merendar	me-re**ⁿ-dar**
piece	a peça	**pe**-sa
pillow	a almofada	al-moo-**fah**-da
pin	o alfinete	al-fee-**nayt**
(safety) pin	o alfinete de segurança	al-fee-**nayt** de se-goo-ra**ⁿ**-sa
pineapple	o ananaz	a-na-**nash**
pink	rosa	**ro**-za

pipe	o cachimbo	ca-**shee**ⁿ-boo
place	lugar	loo-**gar**
plan	o plano	**pla**-noo
(sticking) plaster	o adesivo	a-de-**see**-voo
plastic	o plástico	**plash**-tee-koo
plate	o prato	**prah**-too
platform	a plataforma	pla-ta-**for**-ma
play (to)	jogar	zhoo-**gar**
play	a peça de teatro	**pe**-sa de tee-**ah**-troo
player	o jogador	zhoo-ga-**dohr**
please	por favor, faz favor	poor fa-**vohr**, fash fa-**vohr**
plug *bath*	o tampão	taⁿ-**pow**ⁿ
plug *electric*	a tomada	too-**mah**-da
plum	a ameixa	a-**may**-ee-sha
pocket	o bolso	**bohl**-soo
point	a ponta	**po**ⁿ-ta
poisonous	venenoso	ve-ne-**noh**-zoo
policeman	o polícia	poo-**lee**-see-a
police station	a esquadra de polícia	esh-**kwad**-ra de poo-**lee**-see-a
poor	pobre	**po**-bre
popular	popular	po-poo-**lar**

pork	o porco	**pohr**-koo
port	o porto	**pohr**-too
porter	o porteiro	poor-**tay**-ee-roo
Portugal	Portugal	poor-too-**gal**
Portuguese	português	poor-too-**gaysh**
possible	possível	poo-**see**-vel
post (to)	remeter	re-me-**tair**
post box	o marco postal	**mar**-koo poosh-**tal**
postcard	o bilhete postal	bee-**llyayt** poosh-**tal**
post office	os correios	koo-**ray**-yoosh
poste restante	a posta restante	**posh**-ta res-**ta^{n}t**
potato	a batata	ba-**tah**-ta
pound	a libra	**lee**-bra
prefer (to)	preferir	pre-fe-**reer**
prepare (to)	preparar	pre-pa-**rar**
prescription	a receita	re-**say**-ee-ta
present *gift*	o presente	pre-**ze^{n}t**
press (to)	passar a ferro	pa-**sar** a **fe**-roo
pretty	bonito	boo-**nee**-too
price	o preço	**pray**-soo
private	particular	par-tee-koo-**lar**
problem	o problema	proo-**ble**-ma
profession	a profissão	proo-fee-**sow^n**

programme	o programa	proo-**gra**-ma
promise (to)	prometer	proo-me-**tair**
pull (to)	tirar	tee-**rar**
pure	puro	**poo**-roo
purse	a bolsa	**bohl**-sa
push (to)	empurrar	e^n-poo-**rar**
put (to)	pôr	pohr
pyjamas	o pijama	pee-**zha**-ma

Q

quality	a qualidade	kwa-lee-**dahd**
quantity	a quantidade	kwa^n-tee-**dahd**
quarter	o quarto	**kwar**-too
queen	a raínha	ra-**ee**-nya
question	a pergunta	per-**goo**^{n}-ta
quick	rápido	**ra**-pee-doo
quiet	tranquilo	tra^n-**kwee**-loo

R

race	a corrida	koo-**ree**-da
radiator	o radiador	ra-dee-a-**dohr**
radio	o rádio	**rah**-dee-oo
railway	o caminho de ferro	ka-**mee**-nyoo de **fe**-roo

rain	a chuva	**shoo**-va
(it is) raining	chove	shov
raincoat	o impermeável	een-per-mee-**ah**-vel
rangefinder	o telémetro	te-**le**-me-troo
rare *unusual*	raro	**ra**-roo
raw	cru	kroo
razor	a navalha de barba	na-**va**-lya de **bar**-ba
razor blades	as lâminas de barbear	**la**-mee-nash de bar-bee-**ar**
read (to)	ler	layr
ready	pronto	**pron**-too
real	real	ree-**al**
really	realmente	ree-al-**ment**
reason	a razão	ra-**sown**
receipt	o recibo	re-**see**-boo
receive (to)	receber	re-se-**bair**
recent	recente	re-**sent**
recommend (to)	recomendar	re-koo-men-**dar**
record	o disco	**deesh**-koo
red	vermelho	ver-**may**-llyoo
refreshment room	a cantina	kan-**tee**-na
register (to)	registar	re-zheesh-**tar**
registered mail	a carta registada	**kar**-ta re-zheesh-**ta**-da

remember (to)	recordar	re-koor-**dar**
rent (to)	alugar	a-loo-**gar**
repair	reparar	re-pa-**rar**
repeat (to)	repetir	re-pe-**teer**
reply (to)	responder	res-po^n-**dair**
reply paid	resposta paga	res-**pos**-ta **pah**-ga
reservation	a reserva	re-**zair**-va
reserve (to)	reservar	re-zair-**var**
reserved	reservado	re-zair-**vah**-doo
restaurant	o restaurante	resh-tow-**ra**^{n}t
restaurant car	o vagão restaurante	va-**gow**^{n} resh-tow-**ra**^{n}t
return (to)	regressar	re-gre-**sar**
Rhodesia	a Rodésia	roo-**de**-zee-a
Rhodesian	rodesiano	roo-de-zee-**a**-noo
rib	a costela	koosh-**te**-la
ribbon	a fita	**fee**-ta
rice	o arroz	a-**rohsh**
rifle	a espingarda	esh-pee^n-**gar**-da
right *opp. left*	direito	dee-**ray**-ee-too
ring	o anel	a-**nel**
river	o rio	**ree**-oh
road	a estrada	esh-**trah**-da
roasted	assado	a-**sah**-doo

rock	a rocha	**ro**-sha
roll *bread*	o pãozinho	pow^n-**zee**-nyoo
rollers *hair*	os rolos de cabelo	**roh**-loosh de ka-**bay**-loo
room	o quarto	**kwar**-too
rope	a corda	**kor**-da
round	redondo	re-do^n-doo
rowing boat	o barco de remos	**bar**-koo de ray-moosh
rubber	a borracha	boo-**rah**-sha
rubbish	o lixo	**lee**-shoo
run (to)	correr	koo-**rair**

S

safe	o seguro	se-**goo**-roo
salad	a salada	sa-**lah**-da
salesgirl	a vendedora	ve^n-de-**dohr**-a
salesman	o vendedor	ve^n-de-**dohr**
salt	o sal	sal
salt water	a água salgada	a-gwa sal-**gah**-da
same	mesmo	**mayzh**-moo
sand	a areia	a-**ray**-ya
sandals	as sandálias	sa^n-**dah**-lee-ash
sandwich	a sande	sa^{n}d

sanitary towels	as toalhas sanitárias	too-**a**-llyash sa-nee-**tah**-ree-ash
Saturday	sábado	**sa**-ba-doo
sauce	o môlho	**moh**-llyoo
sausage	a salsicha	sal-**see**-sha
say (to)	dizer	dee-**zair**
scald (to)	queimar-se	kay-ee-**mar**-se
scarf	o cachecol	kash-**kol**
scent	o perfume	per-**foom**
school	a escola	esh-**ko**-la
scissors	a tesoura	te-**zoh**-ra
Scotland	a Escócia	esh-**ko**-see-a
Scottish	escocês	esh-koo-**saysh**
sculpture	a escultura	esh-koo-**too**-ra
sea	o mar	mar
sea food	o marisco	ma-**rees**-koo
seasick	enjoado	e^n-zhoo-**ah**-do
season	a temporada	te^n-poo-**rah**-da
seat	o assento	a-**se**^{n}-too
second	segundo	se-**goo**^{n}-doo
second class	segunda classe	se-**goo**^{n}-da klas
sedative	o sedativo	se-da-**tee**-voo
see (to)	ver	vair
seem (to)	parecer	pa-re-**sair**

self service	o auto serviço	ow-too ser-**vee**-soo
sell (to)	vender	ve^n-**dair**
send (to)	enviar	e^n-vee-**ar**
separate	separado	se-pa-**rah**-doo
September	setembro	se-**te**^{n}-broo
serious	sério	**sair**-ee-oo
serve (to)	servir	ser-**veer**
service	o serviço	ser-**vee**-soo
set *hair*	a mise	meez
several	vários	**var**-ee-oosh
sew (to)	coser	koo-**zair**
shade *colour*	matiz	ma-**teesh**
shade *sun*	a sombra	**so**^{n}-bra
shallow	pouco profundo	**poh**-koo proo-**foo**^{n}-doo
shampoo	o shampoo	sha^n-poo
shape	a forma	**fohr**-ma
share	repartir	re-par-**teer**
sharp	agudo	a-**goo**-doo
shave (to)	barbear	bar-bee-**ar**
shaving brush	o pincel de barba	pee^n-**sel** de **bar**-ba
shaving cream	o creme de barba	krem de **bar**-ba
she	ela	e-lah
sheet	o lençol	le^n-**sol**

shell	a concha	**ko**n-sha
sherry	o vinho de Xerez	**vee**-nyoo de she-**res**
shine (to)	brilhar	bree-**llyar**
shingle *beach*	as pedrinhas	pe-**dree**-nyash
ship	o barco	**bar**-koo
shipping line	a linha marítima	**lee**-nya ma-**ree**-tee-ma
shirt	a camisa	ka-**mee**-za
shoelaces	os atacadores	a-ta-ka-**dor**-esh
shoes	os sapatos	sa-**pah**-toosh
shoe shop	a sapataria	sa-pa-ta-**ree**-a
shop	a loja	**lo**-zha
short	curto	**koor**-too
shorts	os calções	kal-**soy**n**sh**
shoulder	o ombro	**o**n-broo
show	o espectáculo	esh-pe-**ta**-koo-loo
show (to)	mostrar	moosh-**trar**
shower	o duche	**doo**-she
shut (to)	fechar	fe-**shar**
shut *p.p.*	fechado	fe-**shah**-doo
sick	doente	doo-**e**n**t**
side	o lado	**lah**-doo
sights	os lugares de interêsse	loo-**garsh** de ee**n**-te-**rays**
silk	a seda	**say**-da

silver	a prata	**prah**-ta
simple	simples	**see**n-plesh
since	desde	**dayzh**-de
single	único	**oo**-nee-koo
single room	o quarto individual	**kwar**-too een-di-vee-doo-**al**
sister	a irmã	**eer**-man
sit, sit down (to)	sentar-se	sen-**tar**-se
size	o tamanho	ta-**ma**-nyoo
skid (to)	patinar	pa-tee-**nar**
sky	o céu	se-**oo**
sleep (to)	dormir	door-**meer**
sleeping bag	o saco de dormir	**sa**-koo de door-**meer**
sleeve	a manga	**ma**n-ga
slice	a porção	poor-**sow**n
slip	a combinação	kon-bee-na-**sow**n
slippers	os chinelos	shee-**ne**-loosh
slow	lento	**le**n-too
small	pequeno	pe-**kay**-noo
smart	elegante	e-le-**ga**nt
smell (to)	cheirar	shay-ee-**rar**
smoke (to)	fumar	foo-**mar**
(no) smoking	proibido fumar	proo-ee-**bee**-doo foo-**mar**

snack	a merenda	me-re^n-da
snow	a neve	nev
(it is) snowing	está a nevar	esh-**tah** a ne-**var**
so	assim	a-see^n
soap	o sabão	sa-**bow**^{n}
soap powder	o sabão em pó	sa-**bow**^{n} en po
socks	as peúgas	pee-**oo**-gash
soda water	a soda	**so**-da
sold	vendido	ve^n-**dee**-doo
sole *shoe*	a sola	**so**-la
some	alguns	al-**goo**^{n}**sh**
somebody	alguém	al-**ge**^{n}
something	algo	**al**-goo
sometimes	algumas vezes	al-goo-mash **vay**-zesh
somewhere	em algum sítio	e^n **al**-goo^n see-tee-oo
son	o filho	fee-**llyoo**
song	a canção	ka^n-**sow**^{n}
soon	cedo	**say**-doo
sore throat	a dôr de garganta	dohr de gar-**ga**^{n}-ta
sorry	perdão	per-**dow**^{n}
sort	o género	**zhe**-ne-roo
soup	a sôpa	**soh**-pa
sour	azedo	a-**ze**-doo

south	o sul	sool
South Africa	a África do Sul	a-free-ka do sool
South African	sul africano	sool-a-free-ka-noo
souvenir	a recordação	re-koor-da-sow[n]
Spain	a Espanha	es-pa-nya
Spanish	espanhol	es-pa-**nyol**
speak (to)	falar	fa-**lar**
speciality	a especialidade	es-pe-see-a-lee-**dahd**
speed	a velocidade	ve-loo-see-**dahd**
speed limit	o limite de velocidade	lee-**meet** de ve-loo-see-**dahd**
spend (to)	gastar	gas-**tar**
spine	a espinha	esh-**pee**-nya
spoon	a colher	koo-**llyair**
sports	o despôrto	desh-**pohr**-too
spot *stain*	a mancha	ma[n]-sha
sprain	a deslocação	dezh-loo-ka-sow[n]
sprain (to)	deslocar	dezh-loo-**kar**
spring	a primavera	pree-ma-**vair**-a
square	a praça	**prah**-sa
stage	o palco	**pal**-koo
stain	a mancha	ma[n]-sha
stained	manchado	ma[n]-**shah**-doo
stairs	as escadas	esh-**kah**-dash

stalls *theatre*	a plateia	pla-**tay**-ya
stamp	o selo	**say**-loo
stand (to)	estar de pé	es-**tar** de peh
start (to)	começar	koo-me-**sar**
station	a estação	esh-ta-**sow**n
stationer's	a papelaria	pa-pe-la-**ree**-a
statue	a estátua	esh-**tah**-too-ah
stay (to)	ficar	fee-**kar**
steak	o bife	beef
steward	o criado	kree-**ah**-doo
stewardess	a criada	kree-**ah**-da
still	imóvel	ee-**mo**-vel
sting	a picada	pee-**kah**-da
stockings	as meias	**may**-yash
stolen	roubado	roh-**ba**-doo
stomach	o estômago	esh-**toh**-ma-goo
stomach-ache	dôr de estômago	dohr de esh-**toh**-ma-goo
stone	a pedra	**pe**-dra
stop (to)	parar	pa-**rar**
store	a loja	**lo**-zha
stove	o fogão	foo-**gow**n
straight	direito	dee-**ray**-ee-too
straight on	a direito	a dee-**ray**-ee-too

strange	estranho	esh-**tra**-nyoh
strap	a correia	koo-**ray**-ce-a
strawberry	o morango	moo-**ra**^{n}-goo
stream	a corrente	koo-**re**^{n}t
street	a rua	**roo**-a
string	a corda	**kor**-da
strong	forte	fort
student	o estudante	esh-too-**da**^{n}t
style	o estilo	esh-**tee**-loo
suburb	o subúrbio	soo-**boor**-bee-o
subway	o caminho subterrâneo	ka mee-nyoh soob-te-**ra**-nee-oo
suede	a camurça	ka-**moor**-sa
sugar	o açúcar	a-**soo**-kar
suit	o fato	**fah**-too
suitcase	a mala	**mah**-la
summer	o verão	ve-**row**^{n}
sun	o sol	sol
sunburn	a queimadura de sol	kay-ee-ma-**doo**-ra de sol
Sunday	domingo	doo-**mee**^{n}-goo
sunglasses	os óculos de sol	o-koo-loosh de sol
sunhat	o chapéu de sol	sha-**pe**-oo de sol
sunshade	o guarda sol	**gwar**-da sol

sunstroke	a insolação	ee^n-soo-la-**sow**^{n}
suntan oil	o óleo para bronzear	**o**-lee-oo pa-ra bro^n-zee-**ar**
supper	a ceia	**say**-a
supplementary charge	o suplemento	soo-ple-**me**^{n}-too
sure	seguro	se-**goo**-roo
surface mail	a mala ordinária	**mah**-la ohr-dee-**nah**-ree-a
surgery	a clínica	**klee**-nee-ka
suspender belt	o cinto de suspensão	**see**^{n}-too de soosh-pe^n-**sow**^{n}
sweater	o suéter	**swe**-tair
sweet	dôce	dohs
swell (to)	inchar	ee^n-**shar**
swim (to)	nadar	na-**dar**
swimming pool	a piscina	peesh-**se**-na
switch *light*	o interruptor	ee^n-te-roop-**tohr**
swollen	inchado	ee^n-**shah**-doo

T

table	a mesa	**may**-za
tablecloth	a toalha de mesa	too-a-llya de **may**-za
tablet	o comprimido	ko^n-pree-**mee**-doo

tailor	o alfaiate	al-fy-**yaht**
take (to)	tomar	too-**mar**
talk (to)	falar	fa-**lar**
tall	alto	**al**-too
tap	a torneira	toor-**nay**-ee-ra
taste	o gôsto	**gohsh**-too
tax	o impôsto	een-**pohsh**-too
taxi rank	a praça de táxis	**prah**-sa de **tak**-seesh
tea	o chá	shah
teach (to)	ensinar	en-see-**nar**
telegram	o telegrama	te-le-**gra**-ma
telephone (to)	telefonar	te-le-foo-**nar**
telephone	o telefone	te-le-**fon**
telephone box	o cabine telefónica	kah-**been** te-le-**foh**-nee-ka
telephone call	a chamada	sha-**mah**-da
telephone directory	a lista de telefone	**leesh**-ta de te-le-**fon**
telephone number	o número de telefone	**noo**-me-roo de te-le-**fon**
telephone operator	o telefonista	te-le-foo-**neesh**-ta
television	a televisão	te-le-vee-**zown**
tell (to)	dizer	dee-**zair**
temperature	a temperatura	ten-pe-ra-**too**-ra
tennis	o ténis	te-**neesh**

tent	a tenda de campanha	**te**ⁿ-da de kaⁿ-**pa**-nya
tent peg	a estaca	esh-**tah**-ka
tent pole	a vara	**vah**-ra
terrace	o terraço	te-**ra**-soo
than	do que	doo ke
thank you		
said by a man	obrigado	ob-ree-**ga**-doo
said by a woman	obrigada	ob-ree-**ga**-da
theatre	o teatro	tee-**ah**-troo
their, theirs	seu *m*, sua *f*	**se**-oo, **soo**-a
then	então	en-**tow**ⁿ
there	ali	a-**lee**
there is/are	há	ah
thermometer	o termómetro	ter-**mo**-me-troo
these	êstes	**aysht**-sh
they	êles *m*, elas *f*	**aylsh**, **e**-lash
thick	grosso	**groh**-soo
thin	fino	**fee**-noo
thing	a coisa	**koh**-ee-za
think (to)	pensar	peⁿ-**sar**
thirsty (to be)	ter sêde	tair sayd
this	êste	**aysht**
those	aquêles	a-**kel**-sh

thread	o fio	**fee**-oo
throat	a garganta	gar-ga^n-ta
through	por	poor
throw (to)	atirar	a-tee-**rar**
thumb	o polegar	poh-le-**gar**
Thursday	quinta-feira	kee^n-ta **fay-ee-ra**
ticket *train*	o bilhete	bee-**llyayt**
ticket *theatre*	a entrada	e^n-**trah**-da
tide	a maré	ma-**re**
tie	a gravata	gra-**vah**-ta
tight	apertado	a-pair-**tah**-doo
time	o tempo, a hora	te^n-poo, o-ra
timetable	o horário	oo-**rah**-ree-oo
tin	a lata	**lah**-ta
tin opener	a abre-latas	a-bre-**lah**-tash
tip	a gorjeta	goor-**zhay**-ta
tip (to)	gratificar	gra-tee-fee-**kar**
tired (to be)	estar cansado	es-tar ka^n-sah-doo
tissues *paper*	os lenços de papel	le^n-**soosh** de pa-**pel**
to	a	a
toast	a torrada	too-**rah**-da
tobacco	o tabaco	ta-ba-koo
tobacco pouch	a tabaqueira	ta-ba-**kay**-ee-ra

tobacconist's	a tabacaria	ta-ba-ka-**ree**-a
today	hoje	ohzh
toe	o dedo do pé	**day**-doo doo peh
together	juntos	**zhoo**^{n}-toosh
toilet	o lavatório, a retrete	la-va-**to**-ree-o, re-**trayt**
toilet paper	o papel higiénico	pa-**pel** ee-zhee-e-nee-koo
tomato	o tomate	too-**maht**
tomorrow	amanhã	ah-ma-**nya**^{n}
tongue	a língua	**lee**^{n}-gwa
tonight	esta noite	**esh**-ta **noh**-eet
too *also*	também	ta^n-**be**^{n}
too, too much/many	demasiado	de-ma-zee-**ah**-doo
tooth	o dente	**de**^{n}t
toothache	a dôr de dentes	dohr-de **de**^{n}tsh
toothbrush	a escôva de dentes	esh-**koh**-va de **de**^{n}tsh
toothpaste	a pasta de dentes	**pash**-ta de **de**^{n}tsh
toothpick	o palito	pa-**lee**-too
top	a cima	**see**-ma
torch	a lanterna	la^n-**tair**-na
torn	rôto	**roh**-too
touch (to)	tocar	too-**kar**
tourist	a turista	too-**reesh**-ta

towards	para, em direcção de	pa-ra, e^n dee-re-**sow**^{n}-de
towel	a toalha	too-**a**-llya
tower	a torre	tohr
town	a cidade	see-**dahd**
toy	o brinquedo	bree^n-**kay**-doo
traffic	a tráfego	**tra**-fe-goo
traffic jam	o engarrafamento	e^{n}gara-fa-**me**^{n}-too
traffic lights	as luzes de tráfego	**loo**-zhesh de **tra**-fe-goo
train	o comboio	ko^n-**boy**-oo
translate (to)	traduzir	tra-doo-**zeer**
travel (to)	viajar	vee-ah-**zhar**
travel agent	o agente de viagens	a-**zhe**^{n}t de vee-**ah**-zhe^{n}sh
traveller	o viajante	vee-a-**zha**^{n}t
traveller's cheque	o cheque de viajante	shek de vee-a-**zha**^{n}t
treatment	o tratamento	tra-ta-**me**^{n}-too
tree	a árvore	**ar**-voor
trip	a viagem	vee-**ah**-zhe^n
trouble	a dificuldade	dee-fee-kool-**dahd**
trousers	as calças	**kal**-sash
true	verdadeiro	ver-da-**day**-roo
trunk *luggage*	o baú	bah-**oo**

trunks *bathing*	os calções de banho	kal-**soy**ⁿsh de ba-**nyoh**
try (to)	tentar	teⁿ-**tar**
try on (to)	provar	pro-**var**
Tuesday	terça-feira	**tair**-sa **fay**-ee-ra
tunnel	o túnel	**too**-nel
turn (to)	virar	vee-**rar**
twisted	torcido	toor-**see**-doo

U

ugly	feio	**fay**-oo
umbrella	o guarda-chuva	**gwar**-da **shoo**-va
(beach) umbrella	a sombrinha	soⁿ-bree-**nya**
uncle	o tio	**tee**-oo
uncomfortable	incómodo	eeⁿ-**ko**-moo-doo
under	debaixo	de-**by**-shoo
underground	o metropolitano	me-troo-poo-lee-**ta**-noo
understand	entender	eⁿ-teⁿ-**dair**
underwater fishing	a pesca submarina	**pesh**-ka soob-ma-**ree**-na
underwear	a roupa interior	**roh**-pa eeⁿ-te-ree-**ohr**
university	a universidade	oo-nee-ver-see-**dahd**

until	até	a-te
unusual	raro	**rah**-roo
up, upstairs	em cima	e^n cee-ma
urgent	urgente	oor-ge^nt
use (to)	usar	oo-zar
usual	usual	oo-zoo-**al**

V

vacant	vago	**vah**-goo
vaccination	a vacina	va-see-na
valid	válido	**vah**-lee-doo
valuable	valioso	va-lee-**oh**-zoo
value	valor	va-**lohr**
vase	o vaso	va-zoo
veal	a vitela	vee-te-la
vegetable	o legume	le-goom
vegetarian	a vegetariano	ve-zhe-ta-ree-a-noo
veil	o véu	ve-oo
vein	a veia	**vay**-ya
ventilation	a ventilação	ve^n-tee-la-**sow**^n
very	muito	**mwee**-too
very much	muitíssimo	mwee-**tee**-see-moo
view	a vista	**vees**-ta

viewfinder	o visor	vee-**zohr**
village	a vila, a aldeia	**vee**-la, al-**day**-ya
vinegar	o vinagre	vee-**nah**-gre
violin	o violino	vee-oo-**lee**-noo
visa	o viza	**vee**-za
visit	a visita	vee-**zee**-ta
visit (to)	visitar	vee-zee-**tar**
voice	a voz	vosh
voltage	a voltagem	vol-tah-**zhe**^{n}
vomit (to)	vomitar	voo-mee-**tar**
voyage	a viagem	vee-**ah**-zhe^n

W

wait (to)	esperar	es-pe-**rar**
waiter	o criado de mesa	kree-**ah**-doo de **may**-za
waiting room	a sala de espera	**sa**-la de es-**pe**-ra
waitress	a criada de mesa	kree-**ah**-da de **may**-za
wake (to)	despertar, acordar	des-per-**tar**, a-koor-**dar**
Wales	o Gales	galsh
walk	o passeio	pa-**say**-yoo
walk (to)	caminhar	ka-mee-**nyar**
wallet	a carteira	kar-tay-ee-ra

want (to)	querer	ke-**rair**
wardrobe	o guarda-roupa	gwar-da-**roh**-pa
warm	quente, cálido	ke^{n}t, **ka**-lee-doo
wash (to)	lavar	la-**var**
washbasin	o lavatório	la-va-**to**-ree-oo
watch	o relógio	re-**lo**-zhee-oo
water	a água	**a**-gwa
waterfall	a cascata	kas-**kah**-ta
water melon	a melancia	me-la^n-**see**-a
water ski-ing	o esqui aquático	es-**kee**-a-**kwah**-tee-koo
wave	a onda	**o**^{n}-da
way	o caminho	ka-**mee**-nyoo
we	nós	nosh
wear (to)	vestir	vesh-**teer**
weather	o tempo	**te**^{n}-poo
Wednesday	quarta-feira	**kwar**-ta **fay**-ee-ra
week	a semana	se-**ma**-na
weigh (to)	pesar	pe-**sar**
well	bem	be^n
Welsh	galês	ga-**laysh**
west	oeste	**owesht**
wet	húmido	**oo**-mee-doo
what?	o quê?	oo kay

wheel	a roda	**ro**-da
when?	quando?	**kwa**^{n}-doo
where?	onde?	o^{n}d
which?	qual?	kwal
while	enquanto	e^n-**kwa**^{n}-too
white	branco	**bra**^{n}-koo
who?	quem?	ke^n
whole	inteiro	ee^n-**tay**-roo
whose?	de quem?	de ke^n
why?	porquê?	poor-**kay**
wide	largo	**lar**-goo
widow	a viúva	vee-**oo**-va
widower	o viúvo	vee-**oo**-voo
wife	a esposa	esh-**poh**-za
win (to)	ganhar	gah-**nyar**
wind	o vento	**ve**^{n}-too
window	a janela	zha-**ne**-la
wine	o vinho	**vee**-nyoo
wine list	a lista de vinhos	**leesh**-ta de **vee**-nyoosh
winter	o inverno	ee^n-**vair**-noo
wish (to)	desejar	de-ze-**zhar**
with	com	co^n
without	sem	se^n
woman	a mulher	moo-**llyair**
wool	a lã	la^n

word	a palavra	pa-**la**-vra
worse	pior	pee-**or**
worth (to be)	valer	va-**lair**
wound	a ferida	fe-**ree**-da
wrap (to)	envolver, embrulhar	e^n-vol-**vair**, e^n-broo-**lyar**
wrist	o punho	**poo**-nyoo
write (to)	escrever	esh-kre-**vair**
writing paper	o papel de escrever	pa-**pel** de esh-kre-**vair**
wrong	equivocado	ee-kee-voo-**kah**-doo

X

| X ray | a radiografia | rah-dee-oo-gra-**fee**-a |

Y

yacht	o iate	yat
year	o ano	**a**-noo
yellow	amarelo	a-ma-**re**-loo
yes	sim	see^n
yesterday	ontem	o^n-te^n
you	o senhor m, a senhora f	oo se-**nyohr**, a se-**nyoh**-ra
young	jovem	**zho**-ve^n

your	seu *m*, sua *f*	**se**-oo, **soo**-a
youth hostel	o albergue juvenil	al-**bairg** zhoo-ve-**neel**

Z

zip	o zip, o fecho de correr	zeep, **fay**-shoo de koo-**rair**
zoo	o jardim zoológico	zhar-**dee**^{n} zoo-oo-**lo**-zhee-koo

Notes

Notes

Notes

Notes